WE ARE
MEANT
TO RISE

WE ARE MEANT TO RISE

Voices for Justice from Minneapolis to the World

Carolyn Holbrook and
David Mura, Editors

UNIVERSITY OF MINNESOTA PRESS
MINNEAPOLIS
LONDON

This collection was created in collaboration with More Than a Single Story, an organization in the Twin Cities that presents panel discussions and public conversations where writers of color and Indigenous writers discuss issues of importance to them, in their own voices and in their own words. To learn more, visit www.morethanasinglestory.com.

more than
a single story

The University of Minnesota Press gratefully acknowledges the generous assistance provided for the publication of this book by the Margaret S. Harding Memorial Endowment, honoring the first director of the University of Minnesota Press.

"George Floyd Was Killed in My Neighborhood" by Safy-Hallan Farah was first published in *Vanity Fair*, June 11, 2020. A previous version of "How Will They Take Us Away / How Will We Stand" by Bao Phi was published in *diaCRITICS*, June 2, 2020 (diacritics.org). "All the Stars Aflame" by Shannon Gibney was published in the Minneapolis/St. Paul *Star Tribune*, June 7, 2020. "A Tangent to a Story about the Smith & Wesson .38, or, Attempts to Be Fully Assimilated into the White American Project Have Failed Miserably, in the Form of a Self-Questionnaire" by Sun Yung Shin was previously published in "granted to a foreign citizen," *Unstately*, volume 2 of 3, curator Godfre Leung, Artspeak, 2020, Vancouver, Canada. "Financial Trauma" by Tess Montgomery is a combination of two articles written for *Minnesota Women's Press* and a public conversation, also for *Minnesota Women's Press*, and was published on tpt.org. The poem "The Pachuco Himself Considers the Audacity of Language" by Michael Torres was originally published in *Ninth Letter*. "The Trauma Virus" by Resmaa Menakem was adapted from Resmaa Menakem, *Our Grandchildren's Souls: Protecting Ourselves, Our Communities, and Our Descendants from the Racialized Trauma Virus* (Central Recovery Press, 2021).

Published by the University of Minnesota Press
111 Third Avenue South, Suite 290
Minneapolis, MN 55401-2520
http://www.upress.umn.edu

ISBN 978-1-5179-1221-5 (pb)
Library of Congress record available at https://lccn.loc.gov/2021028057.

Printed in Canada on acid-free paper

The University of Minnesota is an equal-opportunity educator and employer.

28 27 26 25 24 23 22 21   10 9 8 7 6 5 4 3 2 1

✖   ✖   ✖

This book is dedicated to the memories of George Floyd, Philando Castile, Jamar Clark, Dolal Idd, Brandon Laducer, Fong Lee, Duy Ngo, Daunte Wright, and all other beloved BIPOC men, women, and children whose lives were lost to police violence in the State of Minnesota and beyond.

Special dedication to Darnella Frazier, the seventeen-year-old whose courageous recording of the murder of George Floyd changed the world.

CONTENTS

> **Introduction: Call and Response** `xi`
David Mura

> **About More Than a Single Story** `xix`
Carolyn Holbrook

> **Pandemic Love** `1`
Ed Bok Lee

> **Juice** `10`
Alexs Pate

> **George Floyd Was Killed in My Neighborhood** `15`
Safy-Hallan Farah

> إِنَّا لِلّهِ وَإِنَّا إِلَيْهِ رَاجِعُونَ **Queer Death in Exile** `21`
Ahmad Qais Munhazim

> **With Birthday Girl Blindfolded, Star Piñata Considers His Regrets and Offers a Last Request** `27`
Michael Torres

> **Battlegrounds and Building Grounds** `30`
Kao Kalia Yang

> **Summer 1964** `42`
Pamela R. Fletcher Bush

> **The Courage to Hold Together, the Courage to Fall Apart** `52`
Mona Susan Power

> **Long Live the Fatherless Children** `59`
Anika Fajardo

> **Land Acknowledgment Statement of a Native Virginian** `66`
Mary Moore Easter

> **Financial Trauma** `69`
Tess Montgomery

> **Cross Pollination** `74`
Kathryn Haddad

> **Breath: A Meditation in Uprising** `79`
Erin Sharkey

> **Dear Editor** `88`
Douglas Kearney

> **What Does It All Mean** `92`
Tish Jones

> **The Trauma Virus** `93`
Resmaa Menakem

> **How Will They Take Us Away / How Will We Stand** `102`

Bao Phi

> **Healers Are Protectors / Protectors Are Healers** `108`

Marcie Rendon

> **The Pachuco Himself Considers the Audacity of Language** `116`

Michael Torres

> **Covid-19 and Asian Americans** `118`

David Mura

> **Little Brown Briefcase** `128`

Suleiman Adan

> **We Are All Summoned** `131`

Diane Wilson

> **A Tangent to a Story about the Smith & Wesson .38, or, Attempts to Be Fully Assimilated into the White American Project Have Failed Miserably, in the Form of a Self-Questionnaire** `141`

신선영 辛善英 Sun Yung Shin

> **Today in Minneapolis** `145`

Samantha Sencer-Mura

> **Let Me Tell You a Story** 149
Melissa Olson

> **Here Before** 156
Sherrie Fernandez-Williams

> **Truth, Reconciliation, and Four More Meditations on Human Freedom** 165
Arleta Little

> **Didion Dreams** 169
Said Shaiye

> **A Time for Healing** 175
Carolyn Holbrook

> **Speaking into Existence** 179
Kevin Yang

> **The Weight** 187
Ezekiel Joubert III

> **Four Genies** 195
Ricardo Levins Morales

> **All the Stars Aflame** 199
Shannon Gibney

> **Humility, Sincerity, Banana Oil** 201
Louise Erdrich

> **Acknowledgments** 213

> **Contributors** 215

INTRODUCTION

Call and Response

David Mura

For readers, this anthology of Minnesota writers of color and Indigenous writers will serve as many things. A presentation of the growing diversity of Minnesota and of the many voices great within us. A series of lenses on the American experience. A bouquet of wordsmiths and thinkers, memoirists and novelists, poets and activists. A panoply of witnesses to the year 2020, one of the strangest and most unsettling in our history. Inspired by the More Than a Single Story series of public panel discussions, this anthology is an exploration of what so many people of color and Indigenous communities have experienced in their own lives; it's also an encouragement for each of us, no matter our race or ethnicity, to speak out, to tell our own stories, to own our power.

Editing this anthology has been one of the literary pleasures of my life. Carolyn and I have known many of the writers in this anthology for quite some time. Some we came up with; others we have watched move from young emerging writers to established artists who will shape this state's literary and cultural future for years to come. The skill and eloquence of all these voices speak to the literary necessity of this anthology.

But this necessity feels even more urgent in a time of such deep unrest and discord, in a country at odds with itself in unprecedented ways. There has been the Covid-19 pandemic and its resultant economic hardships; there have been the divisions of the 2020 elections that culminated in a seditious attack on the U.S. Capitol. Locally, there was the murder of George Floyd, which sparked protests over the killing of unarmed black men and women and calls for racial justice across the nation and the globe.

In such a time, the stories of people of color and Indigenous people, their reactions to the state of the nation, not only provide valued witnesses to our present but also speak to our future. So often in our daily lives, especially outside our own communities, we bipoc may hold back from speaking what we are truly thinking and feeling; here these writers are giving you their full unvarnished truths. Many write profoundly and prophetically about the quest for racial equality. At the same time, the writers in this anthology are singular individuals and talents; each is telling their unique story with their unique voice about their unique experience in ways that challenge and enrich us.

Family, cultural heritage, the racial landscape of America—these themes are constantly woven together in these essays. Recounting the sometimes wayward handing down of cultural traditions, several pieces explore the complications of ethnicity, nationality, and family in delightful and surprising ways. Other pieces recount what so many children of color go through in this country, moving from the rich cultural traditions and conflicting ties of their families to the often hostile environments in school and in their neighborhoods. The writers help us understand their childhood difficulties trying to figure out their ethnic or racial identity, trying to understand why certain people react to them in such negative ways, trying to articulate their own feelings of alienation, isolation, and at times racial self-hatred. Other writers bring a broader political context to their identities and stories, through their experiences as an LGBTQ+

person or as a Korean adoptee or mixed-race individual; several pieces, particularly those by Native American writers, explore the historical and ideological roots of racism and social inequalities and how those roots are manifested in present-day America and what we might do to address these problems.

Not surprisingly, throughout this anthology there are pieces that examine how the Covid-19 pandemic has affected the writer and their family, how the racial health disparities have shown up in their community, how the isolation of the pandemic can mirror other social and political isolations.

Besides the Covid-19 pandemic, 2020 tragically witnessed the murder of George Floyd by four Minneapolis police just outside the Cup Foods grocery store at Thirty-eighth Street and Chicago Avenue. A brave seventeen-year-old African American, Darnella Frazier, happened to be there at the time of Floyd's arrest and she took a video of this encounter, which immediately went viral. Protests and demonstrations followed, not just in the Twin Cities but nationwide, worldwide. A significant number of the essays here provide accounts of these protests through the individual lens of the writer and their community. These writers are intimately familiar with the neighborhood where George Floyd was killed and where so many of the protests took place; that neighborhood is where they grew up, where they went to school, where they live and work.

In all the writings in this anthology, but particularly in those focused on the George Floyd protests, the themes of innocence and guilt figure prominently—for the question of who is automatically considered innocent and who is automatically considered guilty is a key element of racism in this country. In a searing piece, the poet Douglas Kearney describes the talk that all African American parents must have with their children, a talk whose necessity in the life of Black families explodes any disclaimer of systemic racism in our country:

As my wife and I explained to our ten-year-olds (who learned explicitly about a then- contemporaneous application of this constant, historic killing when St. Anthony police officer Jeronimo Yanez murdered Philando Castile): it isn't that law enforcement is simply disinterested in protecting Black people, but that U.S. Culture/Law dictate that our very presence is the thing they are meant to protect against . . . .

That White Supremacy put me in a position to make this a reasonable conversation to have with my then–six-year-olds is a violence I will never forgive. I will go to work carrying it. I will share social space carrying it. I will form friendships carrying it. Yet I will not forgive it.

In the days following the murder of George Floyd, in a letter on the *Star Tribune* editorial page, a teacher from a North Side Minneapolis school, Olivia Rodriguez, wrote that when she asked her class what America means to them, their responses jolted her:

Nearly 100 percent of my class wrote about their fear of police and police brutality. In seventh-grade words, they expressed unjust behaviors by authorities towards them. They are 12 and 13 years old. They do not need this weight on their shoulders right now. Their goals should be learning and being a kid. I sat down at my desk and sobbed thinking of what my students go through on a daily basis while they are walking, playing and talking while black.

No matter their ostensible subject, the bipoc writers in this anthology understand that their experiences and identities reflect a constant struggle against racial inequality, a struggle that began when the English colonists first encountered the people who occupied this land and when in 1619, a ship carrying twenty enslaved Africans landed in the colony of Virginia.

In their own ways, all the writers in this collection are witnesses to history, whether it be the more recent history of 2020 or the histories of their communities within the American story. Too often, our American story has been told from a single viewpoint, a viewpoint that diminished or occluded or silenced the history and voices of Black and Indigenous people, of people of color. In order to truly understand who we have been as a country, who we are now, and who we are becoming, we need voices like those of the writers here.

Still the question remains: out of so many different voices, out of such diversity, how do we form a common vision, how do we come together to create a society that is truly democratic and truly just, that provides a space and opportunity for all of us to thrive?

To address this complicated question, I want to end with a passage on identity by the great African American writer James Baldwin:

> The question of identity is a question involving the most profound panic—a terror as primary as the nightmare of the mortal fall. This question can scarcely be said to exist among the wretched, who know, merely, that they are wretched and who bear it day by day—it is a mistake to suppose that the wretched do not know that they are wretched; nor does this question exist among the splendid, who know, merely, that they are splendid, and who flaunt it, day by day: it is a mistake to suppose that the splendid have any intention of surrendering their splendor. An identity is questioned only when it is menaced, as when the mighty begin to fall, or when the wretched begin to rise, or when the stranger enters the gates, never, thereafter, to be a stranger: the stranger's presence making *you* the stranger, less to the stranger than to yourself. Identity would seem to be the garment with which one covers the nakedness of the self; in which case, it is best that the garment be loose, a little like the robes of the desert, through which robes one's nakedness can always be felt, and sometimes, discerned. This trust in one's nakedness is all that gives one the power to change one's robes.

From America's inception, the confrontation between white settlers and Native Americans, between white slave owners and their Black slaves, have engendered questions of identity, of who we are as a nation. And now, for many, each day in America, a stranger walks into our village, or we are a stranger walking into someone else's village. The appearance of the stranger, Baldwin maintains, challenges our own way of looking at our village, but at the same time the stranger also looks at us differently from the way we see ourselves. And thus, we must question our own identity in ways we have not before.

Again this can be a terrifying proposition, and it certainly was for the Indigenous people who resided in America when confronted with colonizers who took their land and wanted to exterminate them. But our present-day encounters with our fellow Americans can involve a very different process. We can look at the stranger as a fellow human being, a fellow traveler, a fellow American. We can choose to learn from the stranger, learn a different language, a different culture, a different history. And we can comfort ourselves by the fact that this process has always been occurring in America. And in so many cases, such encounters and the exchanges they have catalyzed, have only made us stronger, more resilient, more creative and innovative, more capable of making connections with the rest of the world outside America—that is, if we let that stranger into our village, into our nation, and indeed, into our hearts.

Several years ago, I was asked by *The Nation* magazine to write on Minnesota for an anthology of writers commenting on their states. Back in the 1920s, *The Nation* did a similar anthology, and Sinclair Lewis, the Nobel Prize–winning novelist from Sauk Centre, wrote about Minnesota. In his essay, Lewis commented on the "strange new immigrants, the Swedes." Native Americans and the enslaved Africans have been central to the America story from its beginning; but we have also always been a country of immigrants, whether they were my Japanese grandparents or the Swedes and other Scandinavians who settled in Minnesota, or the Somali, Mexican, Vietnamese,

Hmong, Lebanese, South Asian, Liberian, and other immigrants who have also settled here.

Diversity is our strength. Each new voice who becomes part of America is our strength. The writers in this anthology provide us with individualized portraits of who we are, and in doing so they can help us to know each other, our neighbors, our fellow citizens. These writers prove we are indeed more than a single story.

ABOUT MORE THAN A SINGLE STORY

Carolyn Holbrook

The book you are holding grows out from the first five years of More Than a Single Story (www.morethanasinglestory.com), a series of panel discussions and public conversations in the Twin Cities that I created to offer a platform for Black, Indigenous, and People of Color writers and arts activists to discuss issues of importance to us in our own words and in our own voices.

More Than a Single Story was inspired when I invited several members of my writing group, Twin Cities Black Women Writing, to join me in a reading at a local bookstore. During the Q&A, a white audience member expressed surprise that we did not all sound alike and that we wrote about a great variety of topics rather than one or two topics that are expected of us. My first thought was "Damn! Did she really say that?" But I had to admit that, unfortunately, this is a view that is too often held by members of the dominant culture.

The woman's comment made me resolve to find a way to add my voice to the voices of others who are working to change that perception. The opportunity came when I was awarded a Minnesota State Arts Board Artist Initiative grant in 2015. A requirement of this grant is that recipients must give a community presentation. I wanted my presentation to be more impactful than simply giving a reading, but I wasn't sure what the presentation could be. Then I attended a panel discussion led by author/teacher/activist David Mura during a conference at the Loft Literary Center on youth writing. I knew then what my public event would be.

I designed a series of three panel discussions that featured women of African descent who live in Minnesota, and the Loft graciously hosted us. The first panel featured African American women; the second, women with Caribbean backgrounds; and the third was with East African and West African women. I named the series More Than a Single Story, a title based loosely on Nigerian novelist Chimamanda Ngozi Adichie's well-known TED Talk "The Danger of a Single Story," which warns against fostering stereotypes by treating one story of a people as their only story. I had no idea how the series would be received. I was pleasantly surprised when audiences filled the auditorium for all three panels.

The success of the first year showed me that there is a need for such discussions. I expanded the program, focusing on specific topics and inviting writers from across the BIPOC communities to participate in our panels, creating opportunities for us to talk openly and cross-culturally about issues that impact our lives but are not typically discussed in depth or authentically in public settings.

Recognizing that the lack of acknowledgment of our issues only perpetuates cycles of cultural trauma, More Than a Single Story continues to engage both prominent and emerging writers and arts activists in conversations on a variety of topics: Ambiguous Loss, Reclaiming Our Bodies, Rituals and Cultural Stories That Sustain Us, Reclaiming Our Food, Finding Courage in These Dark Times, How Historical Trauma Affects Our Financial Health, Transracial and Transnational Adoption, and Mental Health in Indigenous and Communities of Color, to name a few.

In the third year of the program, I invited David Mura to design a series of cross-cultural discussions where men discuss topics pertinent to them. This project brought together male artists, social activists, educators, and community leaders in discussions on how men in Black, Indigenous, and People of Color communities view themselves, the role of masculinity in their individual and community lives, and the expectations, projections, and stereotypes they face in this society. In Visions of the Future for Men of Color, panelists critiqued versions of toxic masculinity and explored new models to pass on to and heal future generations. In Young Men of Color: A Dialogue between Generations, men discussed the oppressive and life-threatening difficulties facing young BIPOC men and strategies to help them thrive and help others.

Given that accessibility is one of my personal values, More Than a Single Story has partnerships with several venues where discussions are presented in order to try to reach the widest possible audience at low cost to audience members. I am thankful to the Loft Literary Center; Minneapolis, Saint Paul, and Ramsey County libraries; and Wisdom Ways Center for Spirituality—all whose enthusiastic partnership includes financial support, use of their venues, and help with publicity. Also, without the voters of Minnesota who support the arts through the Minnesota State Arts Board and the Metropolitan Regional Arts Council, we would not have been able to share so many voices, reach so many audiences both inside and outside our communities.

Since the Covid-19 pandemic we, like pretty much everyone, had to revise our programming. We have found that offering our programs virtually has opened the door for greater participation. We are able to include panelists and audiences who are outside Minnesota. And now we are offering writing workshops on the topics of our panel discussions.

When I first decided to put this anthology together, I knew I wanted to work with David Mura. In our own different ways, we have both done much through the years to serve our community. Some refer to us as *Godparents* of the Twin Cities BIPOC literary community.

Our initial plan was to invite writers to focus on the topics we have presented in our public panels. The pandemic, followed by the murder of George Floyd, expanded our vision. No longer could we stay focused only on the topics presented in the first five years of the program.

As David pointed out in his introduction, in their own ways all the writers in this volume are witnesses to history, whether it is the events of 2020 or the histories of their communities within Minnesota and the broader American story, with themes of family, cultural heritage, and the racial landscapes of our country woven throughout.

There *is* more than a single story in Minnesota—and it is the multitude of our stories that is our greatest strength.

PANDEMIC LOVE

Ed Bok Lee

1.

Past midnight, as if drunk on moonlight, at least three birds in several trees keep conversing so boldly, you could roll the dizzying textures of their notes up into a map where poems of joy and lament folded laterally, then longitudinally, get pressed and sent off in breeze-sized envelopes to a thousand other species with little hope of comprehension.

2.

Lately, I also eavesdrop on the encoding far below my dreams.

So far, I've learned: I don't want to die any more than all songs and laughter want to end. Yet I don't want to live forever.

I'm saying I want to keep traveling this archipelago of life and death, leaping freely from one small moment to the next. I want to sleep peacefully inside each of my flaws without first having to get sick.

Whatever makes us smile, hug, kiss, share food with beloved strangers, invent songs and sometimes even belly-aching jokes of death, is *also* contagious.

In fact, everything *but* the physical body dies without this.

3.

I saw proof of all this in the white cop's calm and peace, four centuries of ghostly granite statues holding down his throbbing American knee.

I heard it in every parent's contemplation of late-night sirens afterward for weeks throughout our city. In the hospitals rupturing excess bodies out windows. I smelled a nation of cinder blocks, motor oil, and acrylic, smoldering in each direction from and including the charred Third Precinct police station here in South Minneapolis.

After standing with my daughter at Thirty-eighth and Chicago, the corner of George Floyd's murder—six blocks away from where her life came into being—for a whole day I couldn't eat.

4.

At four years old, my daughter observes her raw, rewashed hands, asks thoughtlessly if rust can grow on songs.

She doesn't know exactly where reality begins and ends. Her consciousness contains innumerable sprouts with tiny petals and bold tendrils.

One day I'll explain that our American President when this pandemic began had previously starred in his own reality show, in which he played a boss who capriciously terminated people.

Eventually, I'll also mention that other American President from a generation or two before, a B-movie actor, best known in Hollywood for his supporting role alongside a chimpanzee named Bonzo; how that pandemic's virus called AIDS in the eighties was rumored to have originated from sex with monkeys in Africa, as CIA-sanctioned crack first hit the streets.

But, for now, she's still too young to distinguish reality from fantasy.

Ed Bok Lee

5.

Within months after the Spanish flu of 1918, people returned to maskless hugging and communal coffee, lemon phosphates, and beers. The reality and fantasy of modernity merged once again and it was as if that plague had been a dream.

6.

Cicada killer wasps are thriving during this summer of sirens. My daughter and I watch as one stings its victim on a quivering tree branch. The predator then drags its winged prey, whirring and flailing, down into its underground lair to lay eggs inside the victim's immobilized body.

We rise from our knees. I listen to all the cicadas' screams throughout history.

Up and down the boulevard, these terrestrial wasps' myriad little dirt mounds resemble landmines on otherwise immaculate lawns.

We move on homeward, later passing the Pioneer and Soldiers Memorial Cemetery where African American soldiers, by some accounts hundreds, from the Civil War are buried—just a few blocks from the Little Earth housing projects for urban Native Americans, in (uncoincidentally) the Third Precinct.

She stops to re-Velcro her sneaker and wonders aloud where all the endless sirens are going. I don't say: to Lethe, or that according to Plato, there were three kinds of sirens who, through beautiful and enchanting songs, would lure passing sailors to sleep, then murder them:

Celestial, Generative, and Purifying.

7.

Whether or not in masks, few people on the street smile anymore. Eyes both eager for and fearful of other eyes. Elderly in care facilities raise a hand to their windows as if already ghosts. Rabbits cowering among brambles wait for a hawk to leave its high, sagging branch. A family of five racoons holds evening traffic up along a Mississippi River parkway.

All night, birds keep experimenting with new forms of poetry.

8.

As a boy, I was wary of how good nail polish remover, or gasoline, could smell.

Later, I learned of lotus eaters, addicts, children in Russia who have a plastic bag and nothing else to hope for their souls. I learned global warming could mummify the earth; that plants and animals, even dinosaurs, comprise the fossil fuels we all now gorge upon.

9.

A million human beings could drown inside their own lungs, as the earth crescendos its wild song.

10.

Tonight, nonemergency traffic has thinned to a whisper. Reportedly, abusers are going crazy with rage, or is it guilt? Some people demand the unhinged be locked up or medicated. Counselors speak with them for fifty minutes each week on a computer screen. Spiritual leaders on TV pray for clouds to descend and wake us forever with their giant wings. Still others believe that the deeper you research everything, the more troubled you become, and the more adept you become at diagnosing everyone.

11.

A voice online speaks of a long-overdue human spring cleaning. His twangy accent is unlike those on public radio or cable TV; his dark

Ed Bok Lee

web observations, hidden by a sarcophagus's hieroglyphics of code and firewalls. "It's about population pruning," rasps the man. "If you can't stand the heat, you keel over in the kitchen."

Meanwhile, across the free and open airwaves, most journalists and newscasters sound as if their words and information to the contrary of the Most Powerful Man in the World were slingshots filled with pebbles instead of stones.

12.

Between "propriety" and "property," which is more indispensable?

If corporations can have rights, what about living, colonizing pathogens?

13.

The other week I stared for twenty minutes at a large bur oak across the street. I stare a lot lately. Its wide largess of leaves swirled and spun in the wind. I stared and stared at its majestic indifference while sirens and rubber bullets fired by police at protesters cracked and lashed less than a block away from our home.

Elsewhere, business owners with long rifles defended their produce, pho, and jerk chicken, because the absent cops seem to be trying to teach everyone who protested against corrupt cops a lesson.

What lingers is not the people with rifles and masks, nor the persistent burning of plastic and chemicals, nor the innocent citizens on their porch past curfew who got pepper-sprayed, but the giant bur oak's timeless diligence. Short of a wildfire or Armageddon, the tree will keep transforming sunlight into food and energy for itself and other trees connected to it through an underground communal network of roots. When another tree near or far in the network gets blighted or infested and begins to fade, the other trees send forth more nutrients to the struggling one in need. When a blighted tree goes dark, the others send energy for weeks, even months longer than we do flowers or daily grace to our deceased.

How to teach my child that within each and every seed's ancient technology is not science, but poetry?

14.

"As a writer, you better not always know what you mean," a middle-aged artist friend reminded me from his home, where he was quarantining. "Just live your life and work as if you're either in or out of sync with the universe's natural unfolding."

Over bourbon, inside our respective homes and screens, we spoke for three hours about the necessity of an artist to love, to be obsessed with finding natural beauty at the heart of the grotesque, and the grotesque at the heart of all human beauty.

Like ultraviolet light, art can illuminate, or burn.

15.

On the phone, my aunt reports a third friend from church has passed away from what started as a tickle in the lungs. I find my eyes once again falling onto the bur oak across the street, its boughs faintly bobbing.

As wind cleanses its leaves, I recall a different oak I once visited near Atlanta. Historically, some nights Black sharecroppers would find the *strange fruit* of hanging bodies. By day, white children loved to climb the Big Oak's limbs. At that time, I learned how humans evolved over eons, tangled and snoring high up in the branches of trees, to guard us from predators while we slept.

Hence, our primal fear of snakes, especially the calmest, most methodical ones.

"They put him to death by hanging him on a tree; but God raised him on the third day . . . ."—Acts 10:39–40.

16.

After receiving the news, I send flowers, then click in search of my artist friend's funeral photos online.

It feels like walking alone down a faint path through thick woods, where all the twigs underfoot are not twigs, but bones.

17.

A virus replicates because it can.

Humans replicate because

18.

"But where did his spirit go?" my daughter asks. May, then June, now July has almost come and gone.

We wander from the corner where George Floyd was murdered, down along the lane of hundreds, maybe thousands of bouquets sent from all over the world. We stop one block north in the open lot in the grass where 132 gravestones made of cardboard, paper, and plastic by artists and inscribed with the names of murdered lives rise up, swaying slightly like a chorus in the evening wind.

"Is he in the sky like your friend?" she asks. Meanwhile, dozens of other people in masks holding phones, candles, and lighters pay their respects. "Or maybe he comes here each night because it's not lonely for him," she says, tightening her grip.

"Maybe," I say, lifting her up onto my shoulders as the darkness clings to our clothes and skin.

19.

You are healthy, strong, and, despite all, despite everything, hopeful.

You are someone's father, someone's mother. You are someone's son, daughter, child. You make art in your own way. In private and sometimes when others you genuinely love are around, you sing.

You like to laugh. You wish you could cry more sometimes. Though intellectually cynical, at your core, hope more than habit gets you up each morning. Or, at least, you believe life could be so much more creative, so much more richly pleasant for everyone.

You open your eyes. Is it despite or because of all she's observing in the world that on mornings when your daughter rises with the sun, her spontaneous, ad-libbed songs contain a beauty as old as the smell of rain?

20.

When Thomas Jefferson drafted the Declaration of Independence, he was thirty-three years old, the age of Jesus Christ when crucified.

We hold these truths to be self-evident, that all men are created equal, that they are endowed by their Creator with certain unalienable Rights, that among these are Life, Liberty and the pursuit of Happiness, wrote the owner of two hundred slaves at his home in Monticello.

These words transmitted/transmuted through his quill's fading fingers—like static-laden voices and music a century and a half later, to crouched, wide-eyed listeners to the first radio.

The spirit of true poetry radiates always light years wiser than its pen.

21.

I saw a tree. It was speaking to three passersby in masks, one holding a camera.

When finally they left, I approached, and stared for twenty million years.

It came and went, over and again.

I did too, from particle to amoeba to cicada to python to angel to seahorse to demon to virus to bat to horse to human—in a wild and vast bestiary of blurs.

Like bacteria inside and all around us, without which we would die, maybe we come and go too fast for trees (or even God) to perceive us, though, sometimes, in fleeting glimpses, we appear in their dreams.

22.

At high noon, the granola my daughter has made almost sizzles on its plate. We leave it with the other items on the table and move on. This summer, hundreds of tents have appeared like mushrooms and wildflowers in public parks all over the city. One such encampment of a few dozen or so houseless people, including families and children, has recently gone up not far from our community garden plot. You can hear them laughing, crying, talking, sometimes arguing, sometimes playing music or drumming.

"Where?" says my daughter. "Here?"

"Sure," I say. We are planting kale and spinach, soon to harvest the perilla.

Meanwhile, sirens keep ruing in the distance.

Back home, we blanch, marinate, and season the leaves, garlic, plantain, and other banchan my mother, a child war refugee, once taught me how to prepare.

At the time, it seemed like art, a superfluous novelty.

23.

I know, a new kind of longing is breaking through even the oldest longings deep within you.

It feels frightening.

It feels free.

JUICE

Alexs Pate

We have squeezed a lot of juice from the stone of racism over the centuries. It's a big ass stone so there is no telling how much time it will take to crush it. In my lifetime the bucket of juice that runs from this stone has continued to accumulate. And yes, it is a stone. Albeit human made, it is still a stone, bereft of any sensibilities and understanding. I guess to be truthful it is more than human made. It is actually made of humans. It is the misshapen, compressed, ossified composite of people who have consciously and unconsciously found themselves embracing each other and their own hatred of other humans for stupid reasons like skin color. They have become stone. And it is really hard.

But we chose to squeeze anyway. And by squeezing, I mean that we ran away from slavery. We fought to escape it. We learned. We loved. We died. And we lived. Langston Hughes's poem "Still Here," in 2020 (in the midst of uprising, political angst, and pandemic), rises in my mind repeatedly. And I guess we are still here because we continue to exist and even grow here for a reason. We are meant to rise. The stone, the great challenge of the existence of humankind, will one day be reduced to sand. And it will happen because we existed.

But the process of squeezing the stone is arduous. There's hardly much you can look forward to. And it requires so much effort. It wears you out. And then just when you feel like that damned stone won't yield anything, bang!—something like the Emancipation Proclamation drips out. A tiny bit of juice.

And from that there emanated a steady, although sometimes paltry amount of juice.

And so we, as a people, kept going at it. Voting rights acts, civil rights laws, desegregation, integration, heroic leaders, equal opportunity, affirmative action, positive activism, a focus on education, and community empowerment. All juice. All of them ricocheting off the desires of people who mean to be and actually feel free.

Sometimes it flows so fluidly that you begin to think that the stone might just give it up and crumble. But no. It manages its leaks to protect itself. While it appears without feeling, it must actually feel something because it will suddenly stop the flow to a trickle.

But guess what? We squeeze harder. Every time. Because why else are we here except to prove that we can bust this thing up? We can raise children who will master their reality. We can excel in every nook and crevice of our world: in science, finance, sports, or intellect. We can teach, drive buses, feed our babies, organize against crime. Yeah, I suspect we can police ourselves if the stone cracks open.

And we can collaborate. Now that's something the stone knows spells trouble. When we build coalitions with others who also curse the stone, it trembles a little.

Hell, there's no way we would have gotten this much juice without help. Hooray for allies! You want that stone crushed too.

But in the end, when I'm driving home late at night or walking down a street or going into a meeting or shopping or whatever and, in a shudder, I feel the presence of the stone, I know it is still strong. Still threatening. And it reminds me to keep squeezing.

I don't really understand it. If I had whole communities squeezing with all their might on me, I'd let go and see if we could work something out.

But this stone won't talk. It must have special powers of mind control because there are people who will defend it. Try to protect it. They'll talk all right. Some people call them Kens and Karens. But there are way more dangerous believers in the stone than them. Still, Karen and Ken are annoyances.

But the stone, it just rumbles. Smashes. Destroys things. It will do that. But it won't or can't just go away.

So, yeah, we have to keep on keepin' on. And we can do that.

I haven't been out of the house, for over five months, except to pick up my thirteen-year-old daughter from her mother's house once or twice a week. Haven't bought gas for my car in that same period of time. Shopping now involves my cell phone and some people out there, who I anonymously love and who will get things and sometimes even cook food for me. I have to squeeze from a distance.

As I said, this is summer 2020. The year (so far) of the pandemic plague and the man who stood naked before us until we asked him to leave. 2020. I know I am writing about history, a significant period of American history. People will either want to quickly forget the realities of 2020 or we will never stop talking about it. I'm not sure which way it's going to go. But I do know that what life was like in 2019 will be nothing like it will be in 2021 if we make it that far. And of course, we will because we always have.

And right now, as I write this, the stone is, like, palpitating in a way that is unlike any time in my life. We squeezers are feverish in our effort. There are more committed hands squeezing right now than ever, it seems. I think we know it won't collapse right now, but you can tell it is feeling the pressure. It has both lost many of its adherents and activated its mental control of its conscious and unconscious protectors.

Still, right now there is too much pain. Too many tears. Too much fear and sadness, which I guess is a consequence of squeezing. Suffering has to happen, as it always has, the more fragile that thing becomes.

For the first time I can say to myself (and I guess to you) that I can't believe that it can keep being a rock forever. Especially now.

Things are changing.

I've had to rethink many of the things that I guess I had slowly begun to accept. Like maybe I had seen all of the juice that so many (and I) had labored for in the squeezing that we would see in the span of my generation.

But I think I was wrong about that. There are new generations of folks who grew up watching people squeeze for mere trickles, and it's obvious now that the stone will give up so much more. And they want it.

It happened in the fog of an unbelievable tragedy that too many saw play out on a Minneapolis street. A man, George Floyd, was filmed being murdered by people who we pay to help people like George Floyd. The police. But the thing is, the police have been killing black men on a whim since I've been alive. Squeezers and relatives of squeezers. The list is too long to recite here, although the new generation chants their names for power. I get that.

And to be blunt, the shit hit the fan, as people said in my earlier years. Friends of squeezers, squeezers and their children, almost everybody said at the same time, "Enough of this."

I've heard from people from other cities wondering why it was here in Minneapolis where the match was struck. There is no easy answer except the lie "nice" just wore thin. People talk a good game here while poor people suffer. While black people are clearly sorted into boxes of inconsequentiality and finally, well, it got lit.

The anger toward the stone flashed and the world has taken notice. People started to see the stone that we had been pointing to for decades in this country. They realized the ground was shifting beneath them. And quite quickly. I don't know how this is going to turn out, which is fine except that it's confusing my journey a little. I had come to accept that the stone was going to be there throughout the days of my life and I just had to figure out how to deal with those moments when it rolled down my street or bumped into my car. Now I have to change again to be relevant in my own head. I'm still a squeezer. I guess that's something.

Along these lines, this year has created another problem for me. It has disrupted my evolving attempt to live my life through a lens of innocence. It's actually a sort of practice. Yes, I said "innocence." And yes, I called it a "practice." I practice feeling innocent as much as I can.

Being Black, I am a member of a people who are largely innocent but who've been told so many times and in so many ways that we are not innocent. Of anything we are accused of. We begin our lives managing the stories about us that lie. It might be a difficult idea to wrap your head around. But, yes, I'm innocent. There is an absurdity to it of course. And if I don't practice regularly, I can still sometimes hear a faint voice within me, which is still trying to remind me that a Black person in America, hell, maybe in the world, cannot be innocent.

But I believe it is very possible. There are only three things to do: diminish the impact of negative stereotypes that cause you to resist yourself (your innocent self); seek to know your good; and try to satisfy it. More discussion about this is required, I know, but it is all I will say about it here. After all, it is only my practice.

Besides, I'm just saying that being innocent is harder right now. The squeeze is on right now. And while most squeezers are innocent, it is difficult to live through innocence while you're squeezing.

Still, the juice *is* moving again. In little and big ways. Certainly, in ways I couldn't have foreseen. I thought the confederate flag would fly forever. I thought some icons of stone could never be pulled down. Names of places and buildings are changing. I thought the virulence of the elements of white supremacy had seeped so deep into the ways of our world that they were light years away from being identified and neutralized. I'm not so sure about that now.

We are witnessing the diminishment of that stone by squeezers who are less conciliatory, less patient, and functionally louder. It is something to see.

Suddenly there are crumbs falling from the rock all over the place. And the juice, not gushing by any means, is in a steady flow that challenges any attempt at predictions, as a new consciousness about the lives of Black people in America is fluttering overhead. All because we will not ever stop trying to free this place of that stone.

Alexs Pate

GEORGE FLOYD WAS KILLED IN MY NEIGHBORHOOD

Safy-Hallan Farah

On May 26, I woke up to the news that an African American man named George Floyd, forty-six years old, was killed twelve blocks from my home—in front of Cup Foods, an Arab American mom-and-pop corner store my family and I would infrequently patronize, one of the only ones still standing in our expeditiously gentrifying neighborhood.

A co-owner of Cup Foods, Mahmoud Abumayyaleh, had received a call from one of his employees that an officer—who we all know now is Derek Chauvin—was killing a man in front of the store, the same man that another employee, moments before, had called 911 on. Abumayyaleh has told reporters that he told his employee, "Call the police on the police. And make sure you record it." Over the next twenty-four hours, the solution Abumayyaleh proposed—calling the police on the police after a young clerk had already called the police—stitched itself into a human centipede of poor crisis management.

Those twelve blocks are shorter than the sprawling blocks on Lake Street, where the bulk of the civil unrest sputtered shortly after Floyd's murder, so they've always felt more like six blocks in my head, but I fact-checked and the store is exactly one mile from my home.

My spatial awareness and reasoning have eroded over time, which is to be expected after twenty-nine years rotating around the sun and still being incapable of unfucking myself from the idea that my home and my body are the nucleus of the universe. I am aware of the limitations of the personal essay, of how solipsistically gazing down the rabbit hole of myself to excavate truths feels trite and performative at best, and at worst, diminishes a story's long-term tellability. But please bear with me, as I try to make sense of the neighborhood that I've resided in since the birth of my brother, Hussein, in 2000, and the joyous and painful memories I associate with this city.

It was an ordinary, lackadaisical late spring day. One of those days where the boredom made all the days preceding it blurrily collapse together in a dizzying way. The air was sticky, humid, and I wasn't sure if it was a Tuesday or a Friday, the beginning of the month or the end of it. I marked the passage of time by whatever was on television. With the way basic cable plans of the early 2000s were structured, there wasn't that much to watch, so my sister Huffan and I enjoyed biking for hours. We could only bike around the block because my mom was paranoid that we'd get abducted, which is an understandable fear that I've now adapted to being a grown woman. We were unsupervised, after all, as both our parents worked long hours to afford the mortgage. Biking proved to be a boon for our unfettered ennui. When biking in circles in the baking sun felt redundant, we kept ourselves entertained the only way a couple of preteen sheltered-but-free latchkey kids could: by stopping to admire the prettiest lawns, taking excursions into our alley, and staring at the passersby walking in the direction of Bloomington Avenue, Lake Street, or Chicago Avenue, trying to guess what their deals were. The longer we looked at our surroundings, at least it seems to me now, the more every detail seemed profound, brimming with vibrancy and significance. The neighborhood became a museum, and we came of age there.

I was the one who suggested, one day, that we peek inside an unmarked cardboard box two doors over, in front of the shady rental building. (What did they rent anyway?) I was known to do that, stick my nose in things. Blithely unconcerned with how I looked to myself, much less how I looked to other people, I didn't quite know where my nose belonged yet. Back then, I wore dookie braids, oversized T-shirts, and basketball shorts like it was a lieutenant's uniform. The look was easier to pull off than the lifestyle that came with the cool-girl, dELiA*s Catalog digs I fiended for; being an unintentional tomboy was more accessible for a chubby Black Somali girl whose family still hadn't hopscotched over the line from "poor" to "lower-middle class" in the Powderhorn neighborhood of South Minneapolis.

My sister and I careened on our bikes, stopping in front of the box. I lurched toward it, wobbling bowlegged with the bike's various tubes between my legs, and looked inside. It was filled with mail. I can't say I knew what my exact reasoning was for being so nosy, but I can say without a shadow of a doubt that my intention was not to commit a federal crime. But to the white man who ran up to us, screaming hysterically, threatening to call the cops on us, we were criminal minded. He ascribed nefarious intentions to our juvenile curiosity ("federal crime" were his words, not mine) before we could even explain ourselves. All my words—"We didn't mean anything by it," "We just wanted to look"—were met with incredulity. I resent that we even needed to explain ourselves, that he couldn't just see how scared we were on our faces, how innocent and pure we were. Fearing what he was capable of—we were familiar with *Dateline* and *60 Minutes,* we at least had the channels those programs appeared on—we booked it home. We kept looking back at him, as we jaggedly rounded the corner, stomping on the pedals.

After that day, I would point my nose toward the sky, trying to appear as incurious as possible, or I would orient it toward the ground, trying to be inconspicuous, invisible. How I looked to my white neighbors if I gawked at a stranger's garden, touched anything in stores, or sustained eye contact with a random person for too long may not have mattered before, but now it did. I became acutely aware, though I didn't have the language at the time, that white people possess a sort of social-emotional illiteracy, a blind spot, that impairs their ability to read the expressions on Black faces. Fear in our eyes is criminality, girly busybodyness is untrustworthiness, and everything a Black person does is suspicious and racially coded. The clinical term for this is *agnosia*, which is usually caused by brain damage.

Minneapolis, my beautiful backyard museum, has exposed me to many kinds of people, so many kinds of *white people* in particular. I still can't, after all these years, say with certainty that all white people in Minneapolis are one way, but at the same time, the act of qualifying general statements about white people is a fool's errand, and I like to save my futile optimism for more important things, like the possibility of Rilo Kiley getting back together. I suppose if I had to accurately quantify how many white people I am specifically referring to, "almost all white people" would be more apt. But "almost all white people" is clunky, imprecise, in the specter of institutional racism. It doesn't roll off the tongue the way compact, sweeping pronouncements do.

Most of our neighbors weren't like the man my sister and I encountered that day, but we learned that was only because that man didn't know *us*. The ones who knew us assigned an infantilizing immigrant nobility to us; we could do no wrong in their eyes because of our hardworking African parents, which sounds wonderful at first, but not for all the people on the other side of that psychic barrier, or on the other side of the city, who they *don't* know. On many occasions, my mother had to plead with our neighbor, let's call her Emma—a geriatric white woman who looks like, with the right wig, Kathy Bates could play her in a movie—to not call the cops on the Black boyfriends of the two white neighbor girls across the alleyway. She couldn't see what my family saw: their intelligence, their kindness, their inherent dignity, the fact that they were having fun fixing cars in the garage, not committing a crime. She wanted to thoughtlessly interrupt their fun. Other neighbors, a Desi couple who owned the corner store on our block, introduced me to the intraracial layers of this: they'd make Black customers, primarily African Americans, come in the store one at a time, but my sister and I could enter in tandem to buy our Fruitopia and hot Cheetos because they had encountered us vis-à-vis our parents first. Gentrification later did a David Copperfield–esque disappearing act with their little business, replacing it with an overpriced Holiday gas station one block away.

The intraracial component factors heavily into this city's white people problem. It's a symptom of white supremacy, so the finger can always be pointed back at white people, but to only assign the blame to them is a flagrant oversimplification. A pattern that I've observed over time is that non-Black people of color with any sort of relational power by dint of skin tone or class ambitions are active participants and shareholders of Black inequity in this city. It's not surprising, then, that an Arab American establishment got caught in a game of telephone with the Minneapolis police, tethering themselves to the cosmic chain of fault in George Floyd's death under the knee of Derek Chauvin as other cops watched him slowly suffocate.

Even the Indigenous population here, who have been systematically excluded from upward mobility, occasionally have their centuries-old racial wounds and anxieties—which white people federally, locally, and interpersonally have inflamed—brush up against Black pain and injury, like in the case of the 2013 South High riots. The Somali American students, too, kicked and punched in every direction. Their own internal anti-Blackness, like an autoimmune disease, externalized in the general direction of mostly African American students, even though they were the primary targets of the violence. The local news mischaracterized it as a "food fight" gone awry. My younger sister Habbon, a bystander, who was there when the rioting erupted in her cafeteria, narrowly escaped being pummeled by the misplaced righteous rage of her peers that Valentine's Day. The Brown and Black student population tried cannibalizing each other like a scene out of *Lord of the Flies*, but the pendulum has swung again, and the critical mass is finally swelling toward liberation. On May 28, 2020, seven years since those riots, my sister was almost tear-gassed near the looted Target by a more formidable opponent: the police. When she came home, she told me of the exhilaration of the protest, how she'd left her glasses at home but could still witness the beauty and euphoria of the surrounding ruins: "It's really beautiful to look at. I love watching the flames. I love watching the residue of the ruins of things that once were. It's just beautiful."

The next morning, the same ruins proved to be a Rorschach ink-blot for white Minneapolis, evidence of their social-emotional illit-eracy, of how they can't read the anguished grins on our faces. Had they found it beautiful too? Maybe some did, but the optics—in good faith or not—of the Karen Klean-up Krew that descended upon the city, virtue-signaling with their brooms, seemed a tad askew. At a traffic stop, on the way to move all of the active files out of my mom's office, I stuck my head out the window of our van and yelled in the direction of a white woman sweeping the sidewalk with her chil-dren, "Hey, ya got any brooms left?" The woman, earnestly replied sweetly, "Yes! Do you need one?" Because I hadn't timed the joke and we were still sitting at the stoplight, I yelled back—in the Min-nesota Nice way that all of the locals, regardless of race or ethnicity, deploy to passive aggressively communicate with each other—"Uhh, I'm kidding! Sorry!"

إِنَّا لِلّهِ وَإِنَّـا إِلَيْهِ رَاجِعونَ
QUEER DEATH IN EXILE

Ahmad Qais Munhazim

I am sitting here in Philadelphia, gazing aimlessly at empty streets from my balcony that overlooks what once used to be a state prison where thousands of lives ended in isolation and behind bars of a racialized justice system in America. The only distraction is a bee buzzing and circling around me like I am a lifeless piece of meat hanging at a butcher shop. I grab a book to kill the bee, but then I remember all the memories that I have of bees stinging me when I was a child and my mom blowing prayers from the Quran on the bee sting and calming me down. Would I have those memories if it weren't for the bees? I couldn't kill the bee then and I can't kill it now. I put the book down and the bee chooses a flower over me.

In 2019, I moved to Philadelphia from Minnesota, where I spent a decade of my life studying, falling in love, forming my queer community, breaking my heart, struggling in a white academy, and trying to survive the slow violence of exile. Prior to Minnesota, I lived in Afghanistan, where I was born and raised.

I was hoping that moving to Philadelphia would give my worn-out exiled body a break to rest. But then the pandemic happened. The Covid-19 lockdown has made me think about life and death, freedom and unfreedom, exile and home. The lockdown has made me think about the stories and lives of prisoners behind this tall colorless wall that I live across from, more so than ever before. What did they do all day long? Did they feel the tightness I feel inside my chest? Did they also have some high and some low moments throughout the day? How many queer and trans people lived and died behind those walls? I am thinking about people behind bars because growing up in Afghanistan, I always thought I would either end up in prison or dead. It is a thought that crosses the minds of many queer and trans Muslims whether living in times of war or peace. It is also a painful reality for many queer and trans people living in heteropatriarchal societies where homophobia and transphobia are either state rules, societal norms, or both.

The bare streets of Philadelphia, blooming pink and white petunias on my balcony, the chirping of birds in the absence of humans outside, and the rushing feelings of loneliness are all familiar to my senses. Since the beginning of the lockdown, I try not to make connections between my life in Afghanistan and my life in the lockdown of exile. I don't want to compare the war I escaped to the pandemic I am struggling to survive. But I fail. I am helpless at the pull of all these familiarities. From the bare streets to the fear in the sound of birds and dust of grief on the flowers around me, all of this reminds me of the uncertain times I have already lived. In the early morning summer breeze of Philadelphia, I smell death. I hear about deaths of people I didn't know. I hear about people not being able to attend their parents' funerals. I hear about deaths of people I knew back home, some dying in the war, some dying of coronavirus. My mom tells me my uncle is dead.

I want to mourn the death of my uncle, who told me stories of Afghanistan before the war, read me poems of love, and cursed me for wearing my mom's heels. But I am numb. I can't cry. I question if exile has made me heartless. I then notice the bee; the buzzing, annoying bee is back. But this time the bee is sitting on a drop of chai that I have spilled on the table, sucking life out of it. I tell the bee about my uncle and his death that I was anticipating for a while now. I tell the bee about the time my uncle was hit by a cow he was milking. We all thought he would die then but he survived. I tell the bee about the time that a rocket hit my uncle's house in Qala-e-Dasht. My uncle survived but he buried his sister on the plot of land next to his house that has now become a family graveyard. I think of everyone in that graveyard.

Then I hear about Sarah's death.

Sarah Hegazi was a queer Egyptian activist who was imprisoned by the Egyptian state after raising a rainbow flag during the Mashrou' Leila concert in Cairo in 2017. Sarah and fifty-seven other queer and trans Egyptians were imprisoned for promoting "sexual deviance." Sarah was forced out of Egypt into exile in Canada. There, in exile, the violence she endured in her past and the pain of a stranger land killed her. On June 14, 2020, Sarah Hegazi ended her life.

I read Sarah's suicide note left by her bedside over and over. I read it in Arabic. I read it in English. Sarah's last words echo in my ears as I am having a hard time processing a Pride month in lockdown away from my queer and trans Muslim community. Queer and trans subjects in exile carry a heavy burden of loss. Queer and trans subjects in exile live in perpetual longing for love and belonging. The home Sarah left behind, the mother whose funeral she couldn't attend, and the land she was born in haunted her into the grave.

While mourning a queer death and looking at Sarah's last post on Instagram, I see her smiling face as she is lying peacefully on lush grass with dandelions around her. The caption reads:

The sky is more beautiful than the earth.
And I want the sky, not the earth.

Her words feel so familiar, just like the bare streets down my balcony, just like the loneliness all around me. I have heard Sarah's words before. I have heard them before in my own head. I have heard them in my own body in exile lying in bed. I have heard them before while looking at exile's sky. I have felt these words while trembling on exile's earth. In exile, we don't walk. In exile, we tremble. We tremble hoping to survive. I have heard Sarah's words many times as I have tried to mourn a home I would never see again.

When one is forced into exile, from the earth to the sky, from the people to the insects, these remind you: you don't belong. But I didn't belong there either. Where do I belong? Where do the queer and trans refugees belong? Where do the queer and trans Muslims belong? The ending of a perpetual longing in exile has crossed my mind. The forever fear of never holding my mother's weak body in my arms continues to kill me inside. The guilt of not being able to mourn my father's death with my family in Kabul has moved me into a state of permanent grief. And for all this and many more, I have thought about wanting the sky, not the earth.

On June 12, 2016, four years before Sarah's death, I was mourning the deaths of forty-nine queer and trans people who were shot at the Pulse nightclub in Orlando. Most of them were second- and first-generation refugees, like Sarah. When I heard of the Pulse shooting that night, I cried myself to sleep, just like I used to do when I was surrounded by the terror of heteropatriarchy in the midst of war in Afghanistan. I screamed my heart out in my dark and silent apartment in Minneapolis, just like I used to do in my dark and tiny room in Kabul. I prayed for the Pulse victims and their loved ones at random hours of the day and night, just like I used to when the Russian rockets would hit my neighborhood or when the U.S. bombs exploded only a few steps away from me. I wished I weren't alive to bear all this pain, just like I used to when my femininity invited the catcalls and laughs of Pakistani men as I served them tea with my shaky tiny hands on the streets of Pakistan when we were displaced. That night, like Sarah, I wanted the sky, not the earth.

There is nothing more painful than mourning deaths all alone. This is something people across the world have come to understand more so during the coronavirus pandemic. While mourning, one wants to be close to their loved ones and cry with them. I can cry with neither my mom nor my sisters, the kindest hearts I have ever known my entire life. Crying over loss of queer deaths with my family is coming out to them, and I cannot do that. I could never cry with them when I used to live in Kabul, because I didn't want them to question my already questionable masculinity.

Men don't cry is a universal poison shoved down the throat of every boy before they even know their left and right hand. The only family member I could talk to in the middle of the night and pour my queer heart out to was the moon. Every night, when sleep would come and rob everyone off, the moon would come by my window and witness my genderqueer body rolled up on the floor in a corner of the room, begging Allah for a miracle of masculinity or an end to the ambiguous body of mine that caused shame for everyone in my family.

When the guys in my neighborhood harassed me for walking too feminine, when my uncle slapped me for talking too feminine, when my brothers beat me for dancing too feminine, I cried blood out of my heart to the moon, the only entity that never ridiculed my existence. When I read that Omar Mateen silenced forty-nine queer beating hearts, I rushed to the window looking for the moon to cry with me, but the moon had gone hiding behind the clouds mourning. However, the sky came down for solidarity, pouring her heart out and storming, like every corner of my heart, for every single innocent life taken, for every beating heart made silent for every queer person dying in exile all alone away from home, friends, and family.

In her last note, Sarah writes, "To my siblings, I tried to make it, and I failed. To my friends, the experience is cruel, and I am too weak to resist it, forgive me. To the world, you were cruel to a great extent, but I forgive."

How can one forgive such a cruel world? How can one be so giving? This is a queer giving. This is a queer forgiving. We forgive despite the hatred we get. We continue to love the family that abandons us. We long for the home that pushes us into exile. We cherish memories of friends who believe we don't even deserve Islamic burial if we die. This is a queer way of love. Sarah's words have been circulating among queer and trans Muslims and Arabs on social media since Sarah left us with grief for another queer activist loss, for another queer death. The world was cruel to Sarah. The world continues to be cruel to Sarah. Some of the online posts on social media about Sarah's death call on people not to even pray for her. One post says, "She chose hell in this world and she went to hell in the after." Another post invites Muslims not to pray for her. The post says Sarah has committed kabā'ir. Kabā'ir in *fiqh*, Islamic jurisprudence, refers to the three major sins: (1) blasphemy, (2) homosexuality, and (3) suicide. In the eyes of these homophobes, Sarah, a queer communist who killed herself, committed all the three kabā'ir, hence, she doesn't even deserve any prayers.

إِنَّا لِلّٰهِ وَإِنَّا إِلَيْهِ رَاجِعونَ Indeed, we belong to Allah and to Allah shall we return. I whisper a prayer for Sarah and I notice the bee on what used to be a drop of chai on the table. The bee is not moving. The bee is not buzzing anymore. The still bee is surrounded by a few ants, and two flying bees that are trying to get to their lost one. Is this how the bee wanted to die? Did the bee travel from afar? Did my mourning kill the bee? I wonder. The ants are pulling the lifeless bee while the two bees are flying away and coming back. They are probably taking the sad news to the other bees. I wonder if there will be a prayer ceremony for the dead bee.

I wonder if my family will pray for me when I die.

WITH BIRTHDAY GIRL BLINDFOLDED, STAR PIÑATA CONSIDERS HIS REGRETS AND OFFERS A LAST REQUEST

Michael Torres

I'm no hero. I'd be out back
in an alley, clapping a pack
of cigarettes if it weren't for this

thin tissue, this ready-to-die
cardboard I'm composed of.
I regret never getting to crunch

the leaves of late October.
I never got to skydive—
to drop through the air

on my own terms—and feel
my tissue feathers tear away
into infinite blue. That I'll never

be infinite, I regret that. And
that I thought I could be. I'm sorry
for that. I'm sorry for not saying

sorry before. Instead, I would say,
I apologize. I would say, *To say sorry
is to admit being full of sorrow,*

and I couldn't go there. I'm mostly
sorry for being so unbendable
and loud in small spaces.

I never got to see the world. Nothing
beyond the sloppy-footed clown
and the sad magician's last trick.

I was hoisted up as he held many
long, skinny swords like a statue
for Bravery I could never model

my own life after. The circle of kids
he attracted, a bubble of quietly
simmering energy. I too wanted to be

something to be proud of. I've left
my favorite words on my maker's desk.

Find them inside a notebook
with a drawing of a tree,
leafless and guessing

its death, on the cover.
If you see *Gizmo, Gallop,*
and *Dreamt* scribbled in pencil,

tear it out. Ball it up. Start a fire.
I'm asking you to erase every trace
of me. I want to go out like my brothers

before me or like some sad magician
swallowing as many long blades
of light in one try.

BATTLEGROUNDS AND BUILDING GROUNDS

Kao Kalia Yang

My first fight in America was with an African American boy. It was August 1987, a month after our arrival as Hmong refugees in the country.

We had been resettled in St. Paul, Minnesota. The bigger family who had arrived months and years before were introducing us to the city through visits to different homes. We were staying in the McDonough Housing Project. We were visiting relatives at the Mount Airy Housing Project.

I was playing outside on the communal playground trying to catch a bit of wind; inside the relatives' house the adults were crowded together in a room so hot the walls were sweating. At the playground, I'd taken off my shoes on the sand and climbed the burning metal steps to a small platform that led higher up to a slide.

A boy came running to the edges of the playground. He yelled, gesturing to something I could not understand. I shook my head. He walked toward me. I backed away. The platform was small. I could only move so far before the smooth heat of the metal bar pushed into my back. We stared at each other for a moment, angry brown eyes meeting, then he grabbed my big toe and before I could do anything it was in his mouth and his teeth were biting down hard. I screamed. I tried to wiggle free but the pain was piercing, so I knelt down and punched his head with my fisted hands. He moved his head in a circular motion to avoid my blows, taking my toe with it, causing me to lose my balance. That toppling moment is long in my memories, but in reality it was no more than seconds. I cried and screamed for help, eyes to the relatives' door on the far edges of the clearing.

My older sister Dawb ran out of the relatives' house, racing my way, her weaker leg from the polio following the stronger one, yelling, "Get away, get away from my sister!"

Three years later, Dawb got her first kiss and it was from a Black boy. We were all residents of the McDonough Housing Project.

It was a gorgeous day in springtime. We were walking up the hill to Timberlake Road from L'Orient Street. On either side of the rising sidewalk, dandelions bloomed bright and bold against the lush green grass.

A boy's high voice called, "Der Yang, Der Yang!"

When we turned, we saw that the boy was on our bus.

We all went to North End Elementary School.

We were not friends and didn't talk on the bus. But there he was calling my sister's name, so we stopped and waited for the thin boy to run up the side of the hill.

My sister said, "What?"

The boy, huffing for breath, slipped his face right by her face, and then away he ran down the grassy incline heedless of the sidewalk or the dandelions crumpling beneath his feet.

I nearly missed it, standing there beside Dawb, confused by the speed of everything.

Hand to her cheek, she said in a voice half puzzled and half angry, "That boy just kissed my face."

Dawb's was the face that was my friend every time there was danger in our lives. Hers was the face that responded to my fear, taught me how to fight, and helped me become brave.

It was 1995 and our mother and father had just purchased our very first house in America, a little one-story shotgun house with a sloping porch on the east side of St. Paul.

One summer night, Dawb and I were home alone with the younger children. It was nearly midnight, but our mother and father were still at work at the factory in a far suburb we knew as Eden Prairie. We had fed and bathed the kids and ourselves and were all tucked sideways on the queen-sized mattress we kept in the front room of the house.

When our cousins visited, we told them that it was our "guest bed." We referenced the old Hmong homes in Laos and the stories Grandmother had told us of her youth on such beds in the houses of beloved neighbors, sharing ghost stories and the sticky, soft ears of roasted glutinous corn.

In actuality, it was really our bed for the nights when Mom and Dad weren't home and we were scared of splitting up between the two bedrooms we shared.

As was usual on those long ago summer nights in that falling-down neighborhood, our African American neighbors ended and began each week with a gathering on their back porch. The men and women drank beer and barbequed on an old circular grill with rusted legs. They listened to music and sometimes danced. Mostly, though, they talked. Through the thin windows and walls, we bathed in the smoky, deep scent of sizzling meats and the stories they told, cut through with laughter, sometimes tears. In the moments when the talk lulled, we paid attention to the music, loud beats that created a pulse in our walls and the air we breathed and slept in. These evening parties by our neighbors had become the backdrop of our lives.

One night, though, things took a turn when one of their friends wanted to get into our house through a bedroom window.

The younger children were asleep between us. Dawb and I were not yet asleep. We were dreaming into the future, quietly putting into words a fishing trip where we might actually stay in a cabin or a tent—something we'd only ever seen on television. We heard the pounding at the same time, someone punching at the window of the middle bedroom. We both sat up. Dawb got to her feet quickly. Without turning on the light, she walked toward the kitchen. I followed her. She fumbled in the knives drawer and came out with a sharp Hmong knife, its fine tip gleaming in the moonlit kitchen. I was scared of the sharp knives, so I grabbed a much smaller paring knife, the one I knew how to handle well around the peels of apples and peaches. Dawb led the way toward the middle bedroom.

Suddenly, it seemed like the clock ticking on our walls had a life of its own; its steady tick was no more, in its place was a new tick far louder and faster than any we'd heard before. Dawb quietly opened the door to the middle bedroom. The room was bathed in moonlight. The sheer blue curtain from the single big window in the room did little to hold the night back. We saw the shape of a person pressed tight to the window. We heard the screen outside the window fall. We separated, each moving with the wall shadows until we ended up on either side of the window. We could hear the loud breathing of the person on the other side of the pane of glass. Someone was with him.

"Don't do this. It's just kids inside. You're going scare them."

We recognized the voice of the older woman from the top of the duplex next door. We didn't talk with her, but we waved to her whenever we saw her outside. She always waved back.

Her voice said, "Come on, you're drunk. Let me help you."

The man's words were labored and roughed.

He said, "You can't help me. Nobody can."

His words broke. They turned into a wail. We'd seen grown men cry before, tears falling from faces, voices shaking with emotion, but we'd never heard a man wail before outside of a Hmong funeral house, cries coming from deep in the hollow of a belly, rumbling through the heart.

He cried out the words, "Nobody gonna help me."

It seemed he hugged our window tight for a moment and then slowly slid down.

Our neighbor said, "Shh, shhh, shhh."

She said, calmly, again and again, "Everything is going to be all right."

Dawb and I stood there, beside that long, thin window, holding our knives and our breaths until the woman helped the man up and they left our house alone.

We did not call the cops. What would they do to our parents? What charges would they bring against our mother and father who had to leave us each night by ourselves to go to work? The thought of child protective services coming in and taking us away was scarier than the reality of holding knives by a window praying for the gentlest outcome possible.

In the morning, bowls of steaming instant noodles before us, we told our parents what happened. Our father left the table, went outside, and put the screen back up.

The neighbor woman, when she went out to work later that morning and saw Dawb and me playing with the kids beside our mother's vegetable garden in the backyard, waved like normal, so we waved back. She got into her car and opened the windows. We knew that her car, just like ours, had no air conditioning.

Brian McKnight's voice sang out, "My shattered dreams and broken heart . . . are mending on the shelf . . ." as she backed out of the driveway and down the road.

We never found out who the man was or what was going on that night. We were only thankful that he hadn't broken our window. Our mom and dad didn't have the money to fix it—just as they didn't have the money to fix the other broken parts of the house, so all we could ever do was clean and clean and clean some more and hope for the best, put our dreams into our words, speak them late at night to each other.

The summer after that near break-in, Dawb and I got into a fight about the mess in her room. She was enrolled in a summer program. She asked me to clean her room while she was gone. I felt I had done it too many times before, only for the darn room to arrive, always, in the same state of squalor. When Dawb left in Dad's old Chevy Caprice, her head barely clearing the steering wheel, I led the younger kids into the third bedroom, its closet walls heavy with blue mold. The light from the window showed us the clouds of dust wafting across her room.

I got garbage bags and the children and I cleaned everything up, Dawb's clothes, her books, and her pride and joy, her immense hip-hop and rap CD collection. I took the clothes to the laundry and stored the books out in the back shed. I made a big cardboard sign and wrote in large letters in black markers: Special Sales Event!

On the stretch of our front lawn beneath the thick branches of the towering American elm, we sold her CDs for pennies. The neighborhood kids, Black, Latino, Hmong, the single white boy who lived down the block with his elderly grandparents, flocked around us. Within an hour we had made $20 in pennies and coins.

When Dawb got home, the younger children excitedly showed her our wonderful work in her room. When she saw that her CDs were nowhere in sight and asked about them, the children presented the plastic bag full of change. Dawb bent at the waist and sank into the old shaggy carpet, grown flat with our feet and who knows how many others before us, and curled into the fetal position. The children, shocked by her response, left the room, gently closing the door behind them.

I felt horrible but I also felt justified.

Later at dinner, over bowls of rice soaked in pork broth with boiled greens, our mother and father told Dawb and me that they were not happy with us. They hoped Dawb had learned a lesson about mess management. They said I had been cruel.

Our father spoke, his words tight, like a rubber band drawn too far. "If you can't get along with each other, how are you going to get along with the world?"

He went on about how a person's goodness is first born in a family, then a community, then grows from there. He said something about how if we can't even love each other through our personal weaknesses, we would never be able to love each other through our sure mistakes.

Dawb and I were both quiet, eyes angry but mouths sealed, our teenage hearts pounding fast.

One forgettable day, Dawb forgave me when she realized that her new collection was beginning to grow into her old one and she would need my help to gather the laundry and store up the books in her room once again.

As we sat side by side in that tiny room, picking up the dirty T-shirts and shorts, stacking the books, I tried to love the music she shared with me. I couldn't. I had trouble hearing the words; most rappers and hip-hop artists moved far too fast for me to travel with their poetry, worked in rhythms and rhymes I couldn't follow. In that room, though, I knew I did not need to try to love my sister.

All I have ever felt when I watched Dawb in that tiny room, sitting cross-legged on that flattened carpet full of her hopes and her dreams, her ambitions, surrounded by dust motes and breathing in wet mold, bobbing her head up and down, moving her shoulders left, then right to her music, was love.

Love is the reason why I forced Dawb to do a hit-and-run.

We were at our neighborhood Cub Foods. She was parking the big Chevy Caprice. She slipped too far into the parking space. She bumped into the car in front of us. The four children and I were in the back of the car.

We were not supposed to be in the car at all. Dawb had just gotten her license and our parents had forbade us to be in the car with her, but they weren't home, and we wanted ice cream, so we were in the car with her.

The hit itself was a gentle bump, but the white woman who owned the car was walking toward the car when the Caprice got too close. She saw that we were Hmong and young, so she started running toward us, a baguette in one hand, the other raised in a fist. Dawb got out of the car, barely to the woman's breast, her hands up in apology, saying we had insurance for the car, saying our parents would pay for any damage.

The woman yelled, "No, you little bitch. You have no business hitting my car! You have no business driving, being in this fucking country."

The woman was so loud people stopped to look. I tried to keep the kids calm in the back of the Caprice with its windows wide open because the air conditioner didn't work.

The woman screamed even louder with the crowd gathering, "I'm going to call the fucking cops and have them come and arrest you. You going to know what life is like in jail, you little bitch! You are going to die in jail!"

The gathering crowd was diverse: Black, white, Hmong, Latino, Native—everyone was just staring, waiting to see what would happen.

The woman ran back to Cub Foods to call the cops.

I saw it all fast-motioned: the sirens, the arrival of the cops, the handcuffs around Dawb's wrists, the children and I quivering in the back, the door opening, the cops telling us to get out, our parents seeing us at the police station, sitting around a table, probably drinking sugary juice, and the child services person cutting in front of them, stopping our parents from coming close to us. Worst of all, I saw us there without our older sister. I saw Dawb in handcuffs, standing well below the 5'0" mark, trying not to blink into the flash of the cop's camera.

I rushed out of the car, grabbed Dawb by the hand, and urged her into the driver's seat.

I said, "Drive. Drive. Drive away right now."

She shook her head, tied to the idea of right and wrong, of taking responsibility where it was due.

I said, "The cops are going to arrest you. You are going to die in jail. The kids are not in car seats. We are not supposed to be here. You have to drive!"

When Dawb started backing out of the parking spot, all the people who had been watching parted for the car. As we drove out of the concrete lot, I saw the white woman, running out of the Cub Foods, the baguette still in one hand, the other flapping in the air above her head like a broken wing, screaming all kinds of bad words we didn't need to hear. The people continued to stand in place and watch her. A few waved goodbye at us. We didn't dare wave back.

A white man tried to break into our house a few weeks after the experience with the white woman. We were still pretty shaken up, praying to our ancestors for the police not to show up one day at our house, looking for the Caprice and its lawbreaking content: Hmong children.

It was now near autumn. The American elm in our front yard, always the first tree in the neighborhood to drop its leaves, was already mostly bare. Crispy leaves covered up the grass, still green from summer. The curtains at the wide front windows were pulled to one side to invite the evening light and the picture of my favorite season into the house.

I was in the kitchen cooking up a simple dinner, beef Polska kielbasa sausages fried with tomatoes and onions. Dawb was bathing the two older kids in the bathroom. Mom and Dad were at work. The baby was asleep. Three-year-old Shell was at the front window.

Shell saw a person with a ponytail peek into our house. The person pointed to the door, a gesture for her to open it. Shell thought that the person was our Auntie Hue—who also wore her hair in a ponytail. Shell walked to the front door, reached for the lock, and turned it.

I heard Shell's scream of fear. I ran to her.

There was an arm inside our door. It was trying to break the chain on top.

I screamed for Dawb.

I slammed into the door with my body. The hand did not back out. He pushed. I moved. I knew I was too weak. I braced my feet against the wall in front of me and I pushed my back into the wooden door. I thought I was going to crack my legs in two each time the door lurched behind my back and my knees went high in the air.

Dawb and the kids from the bathroom, naked and wet, ran out and assembled in a mess against the door. We were all trying to stay away from his reach. We were all pushing against the old wooden door. Each time we managed to hit the door against his arm, the man outside our door seemed to grow stronger.

Little Shell stood away and cried, her hands to her mouth.

In the end, it was Xue, our seven-year-old brother, who had the wherewithal to run to the kitchen and grab a bread knife. Dawb used the tip of the knife to stab into the man's hands, again and again and again, until she forced it outside.

When the door slammed into place, Dawb was able to lock it. My hands were shaking against my beating heart.

The man outside our door swore and swore and said, "I'll be back for you all."

We heard the sound of a motorcycle roar to life. We watched him go away, long hair tied in a ponytail.

For weeks, the roar of his motorcycle circled our house in the night. The only thing that kept us safe was each other and Uncle Eng's old coonhound chained to the front porch pillar right by the door.

Aub Yeng was the dog's name. *Aub* is the Hmong word for dog. Yeng was really meant to be Yang, our last name. The Yang Dog— that is who he was. He would howl like mad each time the motorcycle made its way around the neighborhood.

The unique thing about Aub Yeng was the fact that he only ate Chinese food. Each day, Uncle had to stop by our house with the remains of the day from his job doing dishes at Ho Ho Gourmet Restaurant. He made sure we were okay before he left for the night.

The sound of the evening motorcycle soon disappeared, though we kept Aub Yeng until winter came and he grew too cold guarding our door.

It was sad when we returned the dog to Uncle and his seemingly endless supply of sweet-and-sour chicken and beef-broccoli stir-fry.

The summer of 1997, a white family moved into the long-abandoned house beside ours. Todd, the father, put up a tall fence at the edge of the lilac bushes that separated our houses.

Across seasons, we started feeding their boys through the fence like pets because they told us they were hungry. The three boys never wore shirts when we saw them. As we fed them balls of rice and strips of bacon, they told us stories.

The oldest boy told us that Todd sometimes killed cats and put them into coolers in the basement. He said his mother couldn't take it anymore. It was the middle boy who told us that their mother was filing for divorce and a protection order. The youngest boy just nodded sadly along when his older brothers talked.

After the news of the divorce, we didn't see Todd anymore at their house.

But on a few occasions Todd secretly came to visit his boys when they were outside from our side of the fence. We were wary of Todd, but we also felt sad for him. On those few visits, he asked us if we'd be willing to listen to his poetry. Dawb was kind enough to stand within a reasonably friendly distance; the younger kids and I made sure to stand always within reach of our front door, just close enough so we could hear his readings. All of them were sad love poems. He told us, "They are sonnets like Shakespeare's."

In the fall of 1997, Dawb started college. Two years later, it was my turn.

It was 2003 and I was a senior in college when the house was broken into. Our grandmother had died at Uncle Eng's house. Following the tradition of our people, we went over often to spend nights, warming up their house with the sounds of life.

We were not home the night of the break-in. The persons who broke into the house came through the back where Mom's garden was. They stepped on her tomato and chili plants, her Thai basil, and through the patch of mint. They broke into a window near the back and entered the house through the kitchen.

The thieves took everything of value: our television, our traditional Hmong clothes, the precious life savings of the younger children, coins in fruit jelly containers from the Asian stores, the family's single computer. They left behind a weapon: a leg of a table with a long nail sticking out of one end.

We called the cops when we came home and found the house in disarray. Two cops arrived and after a walk-through told us that there was nothing they could do.

A few days later, Dawb forgot her keys and knocked on our Latino neighbors' door; they lived in the downstairs duplex. She asked if she could use their phone. They said yes. Inside, she saw our television and our computer and the kids' empty savings containers. The two boys, friends of our younger siblings, were shy and embarrassed, but their father acted normal so Dawb did too.

A few months after the break-in, after ten years in America, our family moved away from St. Paul and life was never the same again. But by then, Dawb and I were mostly made. We had learned how to get along with each other and the communities we lived in and would take that with us no matter where we went in the unraveling future.

SUMMER 1964

Pamela R. Fletcher Bush

In my reflection of the mid-to-late '60s, I've discovered that my mind has filed some memories in a recess that it opens only when it knows I'm ready to remember. Unlike my full recollection of the summer of 1964, I remember only fragments of the following years. They float to the surface when I least expect them. Although I weep when I recall them, I welcome the lessons I'm ready to receive.

In April 1964, as the rainy season slackens, for-sale signs pop up along Barrydale Street. The next-door neighbors on either side move first. Then those across the street leave. By the end of the summer, the Strong family, who lives directly across the street from us, is one of the few original families left. Although Mama and Daddy don't mention it, I realize that we are the first colored family to move into this neighborhood. In our old neighborhood in South Central Los Angeles, everybody is colored. At 107th Street School, all the kids and all the teachers are colored. At our new school, Flanner, Joey and I are the only colored kids in our classes, and none of the teachers is colored. As each family moves farther away from us, I gather they're leaving for the same reason that the Sixteenth Street Baptist Church was bombed last summer. Like Mama said, they don't want colored and white children to go to school together.

After school ends for the summer, the Rushen family moves

into the house on the far end of the block across the street. They have three children: a baby daughter and two elementary-school-age daughters. Rhonda is a year older than I am, and Juliette is a year younger than Joey. I'm delighted to finally have friends who look like me. Soon we kids turn Barrydale Street into a boisterous playing field, where we play kickball, tag, and hide-and-go-seek.

Mama loves to bake pound cakes and strawberry pies to welcome our new neighbors. She and Daddy dress nicely, not like they're going to church but nice enough, and then Mama carefully delivers the treat with a warm smile. The neighbors are happy to get the freshly baked goods, and we become the most popular family on the block. The kids love to come to our kitchen, where Mama offers them Kool-Aid and whatever sweets are around.

"It's a good way to meet your neighbors," Mama tells me one day when I ask her why she takes food to strangers' homes. "I want to know whose kids you're playing with. Make sure they come from decent homes."

I think she's just being nosy, but I guess she has a point. Like her, I too like to go inside people's houses, where I can see what's really going on.

One Sunday afternoon after they come home from welcoming the Van Durens, Mama brings us sandwiches made with Wonder Bread, butter, and chocolate sprinkles that Mrs. Van Duren has just made. It is the first time Mama has returned home with a *thank-you gift*.

"I guess they Canadian sandwiches," Daddy says, picking one up and examining it.

"No, I think she said they're Dutch," Mama says.

We've never had white people's food before, so we kids don't know what to make of this fare, let alone things Canadian or Dutch. We can't fathom sandwiches made of ingredients other than peanut butter and grape jelly, salami and cheese, and tuna or turkey salad.

Besides, chocolate sprinkles belong on cupcakes, like *Hostess cup-cakes* with that yummy whipped cream center. None of us wants to taste this odd concoction, so I return to my drawings and Joey and Gail resume watching Walt Disney.

When the doorbell rings the next morning, I scramble to the door from the bathroom, where I've been cleaning. Mama answers before I get there.

"Hi, Betty!" Eight-year-old Beatrix Van Duren and her older sister, Becca, stand at the door, wearing shorts and no shoes. They look quite comfortable, though I would never go outside barefooted.

"Can your kids come out and play?" Beatrix asks.

I stand at the door with my mouth wide open, never having heard kids call adults by their first names. I look at Mama to gauge her reaction. She looks pleasant, surprisingly.

"Good morning, Beatrix. How do you do, Becca? First of all, the proper way to greet your elders is to say, 'Good morning, or good evening, Mr. and Mrs. So-and-So.' When you visit my home, you call me Mrs. Franklin, not Betty. Secondly, my children are busy doing chores, so they won't be ready to play till this afternoon. Please come back then." Mama flashes a smile and waits for their response. "Do you understand, girls?"

Beatrix shoots Becca a curious look and nods at Mama. "Yes, I understand, Mrs. Franklin." Becca nods her head and grins.

They smirk at me, wave, and flit away. Mama closes the door and says, "Don't pick up any bad habits from those children, Renny. The nerve . . . their parents are much too lenient with them. I'll teach 'em right."

Beatrix fascinates me, and as I clean the bathtub, I think about her manner, something different, wild. She's not like Renee, Rhonda, Juliette, or me, the good girls, or at least we're good in front of adults. I bet Beatrix talks too much, says the wrong things, does what she wants, gets into trouble all the time. I hope she comes back later.

Beatrix is named after Queen Beatrix of Holland, home of her Dutch parents. But her family calls her BK. They moved from Canada to the United States, which means they're Canadian, not American, BK informs me. I don't know what this means, but I just listen and nod my head. She's so different from anyone I've ever met, and I'm glad. She's loud unlike Becca, who isn't really quiet but doesn't stand out. When I meet Betsy, the eldest sister, I notice that BK and Betsy would be twins if they weren't so far apart in age. They act alike, look alike with broad foreheads and big noses, and are built alike, *big-boned*—I think they call it *tall*, too. Betsy is a teenager, who dyes her hair, and smokes and cusses, even in earshot of her parents! Becca is bony with a moon-shaped head that's too big for her little body, shaped more like their brother, Benson. He is the eldest and the only boy, nice but distant.

Benson and Becca look like Mr. Van Duren, *Papa*, they call him, and Betsy and BK look like Mrs. Van Duren. Both parents are tall; Papa is lanky and long-footed. It's too bad that I don't understand Papa Van Duren much; he speaks in a melodious accent, teasing me all the while. I like him immediately. I do understand him when he calls his wife, *Mama*. Mama Van Duren is easier to understand, and she calls her husband *Papa*. I also like her. She's odd looking, though, pale with painted-on, too-thin eyebrows and sparse red hair that may be dyed.

I sit in their living room taking in everything: the two cats, the dog, and the gigantic tortoise. One wall is covered with porcelain windmills. Colorful paintings of tulips hang on another wall. There's also a collection of tiny silver spoons, porcelain thimbles, and porcelain clogs arranged on a whatnot shelf. The coffee table and end tables are decorated with lace doilies and ceramic figurines of rosy-cheeked girls in what appear to be costumes, but are they Dutch or Canadian clothes? It is a comfortable house, welcoming though mysterious.

After visiting the Van Durens, I go home and look around our house. There's a large oil painting covering the wall above our living room sofa. It's not colorful, just a gilded, dark picture of a city. A gold-framed mirror hangs above the fireplace, and a glass, aqua-blue seal sits on the coffee table. On the dining room table rests a crystal bowl of plastic fruit. Against one wall stands a stereo inside a beautiful dark wood cabinet that only Mama and Daddy can touch. Unlike the Van Durens, we don't sit in the living room or the dining room, unless we have company. My family spends most of our time in the den or in the kitchen. When kids come over to visit, Mama makes us stay outside, either in the back or front yard. She doesn't like us closed up in our bedrooms, where she can't see what's going on.

As soon as I step inside the Van Durens' home, I could tell they are unlike anyone else I've ever met. Somehow their home tells me that they are Canadian and Dutch, yet I'm not sure what that really means. What do we have in our home that tells people we're colored? On the chest of drawers in my parents' bedroom someone would find two family photographs, one without Little Eddie, and a recent one that includes him. Other than that, how would someone know we're colored?

When I go to Rhonda and Juliette's home, I don't detect anything that tells me that they're colored, except their school pictures hanging on a wall. Like Mama, Mrs. Rushen sends us outdoors to play, so I don't get much time to really look around their house. I've never had a reason to visit Ricky's and Raoul's houses, so I don't know if I'd find anything in there that would tell me they're Mexican. I doubt I would have even thought about it if I hadn't heard them speak Spanish or speak English with an accent.

Since I don't know other Canadians, I can't tell whether or not BK and her family are like those who live in Canada. I wonder where it is. When I visit her one day, I ask BK to tell me. She asks Papa Van Duren to explain, but I don't understand much of what he tells me. When I ask where Dutch is, BK laughs, and I feel stupid.

"Dutch is the language of the Netherlands, sweetheart. How would you know this? You are a little American," Mama Van Duren says, reaching out to hug me. "BK, you hush. Don't mind her, such a rude little girl. It also means the people of the Netherlands.

Holland, our home [she points to herself and to Papa Van Duren] is in the Netherlands, which is in Western Europe. It's a faraway land, Renny."

"You miss it?" I ask, wondering how I would feel if I were someplace else, far away from La Puente. I've already forgotten Main Street, and I don't remember a thing about Houston.

"Sometimes, yes, uh huh," Mama Van Duren says, releasing me. "When I remember being young like you, yes, I miss some things about it."

"Maybe you go with us someday to see the beautiful flowers," Papa Van Duren says, and I feel better when he smiles at me. He reaches for a book, beckons for me to sit next to him, and shows me a map of Europe. BK comes over, sits down at my feet, and leans against me. Feeling the warmth of her body, I forgive her.

"And here we are now," he says after pointing out Alberta, Canada. He shows me Los Angeles, California.

I can't imagine traveling so far away from home, so I just stare at the map, not knowing what else to say.

It is too far to go to Main Street Church of Christ every Sunday, so now we go to La Puente Church of Christ. Unlike Main Street, La Puente is a white congregation, and our family is one of three colored families who attend regularly. Mama and Daddy don't mention this or the difference between the two churches, but I see it in the singing and in the preaching. These people sing fast, as if they can't wait to stop singing, and they sound bored, as if they wish they were somewhere else. I recognize only a few of the hymns, and they sing them in a different rhythm. The preacher just talks, like he's having a conversation with himself, smiling away. Why is he smiling like that? I thought preaching was a serious thing, at least it was at Main Street, where the preacher looked sad or mad, and everybody looked like they were deep in thought about God's message. In Bible class, Miss Sister Jackson smiled a lot, which I liked, 'cause we were kids having fun; she would smile at me and ask for my answers, and always said, "That's right, Renny. You really studied your lesson, didn't you?" My new Bible class teacher doesn't seem to see me, even though I'm the only colored girl in the class. And most of the people, looking unfriendly, don't even shake Mama and Daddy's hands after the service. Things could be worse, I guess. It's a good thing we're not going to a colored church in Mississippi, where white people are bombing churches left and right!

They recently found those three civil rights workers, two white fellows and a colored one, dead in Philadelphia, Mississippi, killed by white people, who don't want colored people to have the vote. It's getting so bad I can barely stand to see the news these days. When it comes on, I go to my bedroom and shut the door. If it's not church bombings, it's riots in New York and New Jersey. These days Mama and Daddy don't talk about the news like they used to, when we lived on Main Street. And I'm having that bad dream again: someone is chasing me, and when I open up my mouth to scream, no sound comes out.

Rhonda tells me that her father doesn't trust white folks and that she and Juliette can't play with BK and Becca anymore. If I want to play with her and Juliette, I have to come over to their house now.

"It appears that you like playing with them white girls more than you like playing with us," Rhonda says one day when Mama lets me visit for the afternoon.

I do enjoy playing with BK more, but I never connected it to her being a white girl. I don't know what to say. "I like playing with you both," I finally say, which is true.

"Then why are you always at they house, sleeping over and everything? And when you're not over there, they at your house. My mama says it appears like ya'll live in the same house."

I feel angry now and say, "I should be able to play with anybody I want. I like you both the same, so what's the big deal? I'm here now, not there, so why can't we have some fun? Don't you want to be my friend, Rhonda?"

She looks at me as if she wants to say something else, like she's unhappy. But she says, "Okay! Let's draw, Renny. I got me some new crayons. Wait till you see the dress I drew last night. My mama says I should go to fashion design school when I grow up."

Something tells me that at this moment our relationship will never be the same again. I feel sad, on the verge of crying, because I just want friends. Colored or white? What difference does it make?

One August evening in 1965, we kids rush to the television, where we hear sirens and shouting. We watch burning buildings crumple and colored people fight with the police.

"Why are they fighting and burning things down?" Gail asks Daddy. She sits too close to the television, but Daddy doesn't notice.

"I guess they're really upset, honey."

"Why? What happened?"

"White folks do colored people wrong sometimes," Daddy says and turns away from the television to look at me. I sit silently beside him on the sofa.

"Now, don't you feel sad, Renny. It'll be all right. Okay?"

"Okay." I still feel sad when I leave the family room. I shut the door to my bedroom and stretch across my bed to look at the cute clothes in *American Girl*.

I don't have anyone to talk to about the angry faces I see on the television, so when I feel down, I read and listen to music on my transistor radio. Sometimes I write stories of places I want to go to and people I want to meet. I miss Rhonda. She and her family moved back to Los Angeles after school ended for summer vacation. Although she and I stopped playing together like we used to, I felt sad when she left.

The church kids and I don't talk about the burning buildings and the smoke we can see in the sky. We chase each other around the yard, climb trees, and pick plums. But later, when I'm alone, I wonder why colored people and white people are mad at each other. When BK and I laugh and dance at my house, I forget about the news. But when I visit her house, Bobby, her teenaged brother, doesn't look at me or say hello. I wonder if he's mad at me.

Joey and Gail fight the white kids in our neighborhood because of the ugly name-calling, like "Little Black Sambo" and "Nigger."

"All right, now. You kids will have to stay in the backyard or come inside, if you can't get along," Mama tells them.

"That's not fair, Mama. They start the fights," Gail shouts.

"You heard what I said. And watch your mouth, little girl." Mama glares at Gail, which makes her cry and whisper, "It's not fair. It's not fair."

Joey says nothing. He goes to his room and turns up the volume on the television.

One morning, during the summer of 1966, Daddy takes us to the Watts Festival, where we see so many colored people! We see little shops, where men and women sell colorful beaded jewelry and vibrant outfits. We walk for blocks and all we see are colored families huddled together on blankets and kids running around and having fun, dancing to the sounds of the drummers marching down the street in the parade. Then I see Miss Watts rolling along, sitting high in the back seat of a turquoise blue convertible. She smiles and waves at the crowd.

One colored man hollers, "Hey! Black is Beautiful, my Queen. You are black and oh so beautiful."

Black and beautiful. I have never heard those words come together like that before. I cradle them in my mind. I notice that Miss Watts's hair is not pressed straight like mine. It is shaped round and high on her head. I see others with similar hairstyles, both the men and women wearing big, bushy hair. Some women, though, wear their hair cut very short and some are bald. *Black and beautiful.* I feel happy that day. I grin at Daddy, and the light of the sun is reflected in his smile.

The tumultuous year of 1968 brings an abrupt, violent end to Dr. Martin Luther King Jr.'s life on April 4. In the aftermath of his assassination, the news broadcasts the "black rage" erupting around the country. I feel afraid, anxious, and alone. I read *American Girl* magazines to escape the tension of the external world and the silence of my parents. They go to work and send us kids to school, as if everything is normal.

One afternoon, while walking home from school, BK speaks to me in a frantic tone that I don't recognize.

"Get behind me! Get behind me!" She hurries along the sidewalk, moving away from me, and waves at a group of white girls zipping by.

"Hey, BK," they holler over a boisterous horn.

In that very moment, I witness the fiery collapse of our friendship. The shock causes me, at twelve years old, to finally perceive the difference between colored and white. BK is no longer my best friend. She turns into some strange white girl, who treats me wrong. After she is sure that the car has turned the corner, she speaks to me like the BK I used to know. But I can no longer hear or see her. When we get to Barrydale Street, I don't stop at her corner house, as usual. I keep walking.

THE COURAGE TO HOLD TOGETHER, THE COURAGE TO FALL APART

Mona Susan Power

I come from a long line of hereditary chiefs of the Iháŋktuŋwaŋna Dakóta nation, and my grandmother and mother trailed the footsteps of these ancestors in their own activist leadership.

Grandma Josephine is born in January 1888, near the banks of Battle Creek in Dakota Territory. The frozen waters warn her that life will involve great conflict, though she herself carries no weapons but a fair mind and warm heart.

Grandma Josephine sweeps into the world on blizzard winds that claim the lives of many children. Her first breath is smoke. She is born in the long shadow of the massacre at Whitestone Hill where twenty-five years earlier the peaceful village of her grandfather, Chief Mahto Nuhpa (Two Bear), is attacked by Generals Sully and Sibley and their federal troops. These Northern generals are on a campaign to decimate the Dakota nation, remove our people from the Earth. They kill hundreds of men, women, children, elders, tear down dozens of lodges, and burn them along with food supplies in order to starve any survivors. Josephine hears stories of dogs being chased from the carnage, dragging small travois with babies strapped to the poles by desperate parents. She will remember these images, though the awful history is already in her blood, tangled in strands of DNA.

At the age of fourteen, Josephine is sent to the Carlisle Indian Industrial School in Pennsylvania and isn't allowed to return home until she graduates seven years later. Her parents are still living in a tipi lodge but have built a small cabin for her, since they don't know what to expect from this daughter who has lived with white people for so many years. Grandma quickly recovers her original language and becomes a trusted reservation leader, elected chairperson of the Standing Rock Sioux nation in 1946. She hitchhikes to Washington, D.C., during the Depression, seeking to protect the rights of her people. She can walk for miles and loves to dance. She looks forever outward, away from herself, gracefully carrying the weight of leadership on her strong back. But she outlives too many of her children and grandchildren. My mother says it is grief and exhaustion that cause her to refuse treatment when she breaks her hip. She won't allow the doctor to reset her bones so she can walk again. In later years she loses two of her limbs to diabetes. This is the first generation to lose their legs.

My mother, Susan Louise Kelly, is a fighter like her mother. She travels from Fort Yates, North Dakota to Chicago via Amtrak's Empire Builder in 1942—her first time riding a train. She's seventeen, leaving her mother and younger siblings, leaving high school before graduating, because a relative has requested her services as a companion and maid. She'll be living with the only rich Indian she's ever met, a woman whose husband even owns a small plane. Mama doesn't want to leave the reservation and head into the unknown. She's proud, so she bites her lip to prevent tears from falling, looks away to the window. She doesn't know there's a restroom on board that she can use. So she sits in her seat for long, uncomfortable hours, observing the landscape as it rushes past in bleary streaks of blue and green that make it look like she's held underwater.

Mama always intends to move back to the reservation when she saves enough money but ends up sticking to Chicago, though it never feels like home. She is one of the founders of the American Indian Center as well as other Native organizations in the city. She protests the condition of Native people lured to cities during Relocation only to end up in crumbling ghettos. Her phone number passes through many hands, all across the country. Activists hear that our home is a safe place to land if they're in hiding. Anyone in need of a meal and a couch, in need of an advocate, knows they can call her anytime. She is most eloquent when she's angry.

As a little girl I feel I don't deserve these women, to be in their lineage. I'm not like them, though I want to be. I find their courage and fortitude astonishingly clear, as if their dresses are pinned with medals. Unlike them, I am beset by nervous terrors nearly every day. I try to explain this feeling to Mama when I'm little, how I'm shaking inside, but she hushes the words. "No, you're not! If you talk like that, you'll just convince yourself of things that aren't true."

Mama tells me stories of brave ancestors who were taught at an early age to be quiet in danger times, to remain silent as death when they were hunted. The stories shame me, safe as I am sitting on a kitchen chair in our Chicago apartment. Why am I such an anxious baby? Is it because only one of my parents is Dakota, diluting my strength? I am forever confused. I cannot fathom the pain of these other children, and yet I can. Their terror and grief are inside me, haunting my heart. Nearly every night I dream that an angry crowd of strangers is chasing me through a local park, determined to kill me. Sometimes I escape their grasping hands, and sometimes I feel the bullet as it strikes my body. I wake in pain, patting down the area where I'm injured only to realize I'm fine. The vicious mob murdered a ghost.

I've held myself together with what feels like tape and string for more than forty years, though my life looks good on paper in terms of educational degrees and professional awards. I've worked on healing the unexpressed fury of a scared child since college years, when I majored in psychology. My mother has drilled into me that therapy is futile, that a profession dominated by white practitioners will never understand us or merit our trust (which is often true). She has further argued that navel-gazing is practically a sin, that the best way of getting on is to distract the selfish mind, the sullen emotions, through good works. Volunteer. Do something for someone else. Which is terrific advice, until you begin to split at the seams and there isn't enough of you to walk out the door. So I spend decades reading self-help books and writing in journals, in an attempt to cure the growing clutch of Depression. I think of this exhausted grief as my partner. I tell myself I didn't choose him, he chose me. He's a persistent being who holds me tighter and tighter with each passing year, until there is no distance between us, no breath or space or light that pulls me away from his arms. I live in his shadows.

On a morning in April 1973, I find my beloved father dead on the floor of our garage. His loss is a mystery the court declares cannot be solved, though I have dreaded this day since earliest memory, steeling myself against the coming loss. There is great love in our home. There is bitter violence. I've long feared that I'll fail to protect my loved ones from one another, a self-appointed job since I first learned to walk. My father's death brings an intruder, a being who rides grief like his favorite car. He never shows me his face, wrapped as he is in a draining fog, but when I'm older I'll learn his name is Depression. He dims my light and whispers lies. I don't want to believe what he tells me, but he convinces.

In May 2003, a month to the day before my spectacular fail, I dream of climbing the tall aluminum ladder I purchased so I can change lightbulbs in fixtures attached to the high ceilings of my apartment. In the dream my hands are empty of bulbs, my climb mysteriously without purpose. As I reach the top something unbalances me. Time slows enough for me to realize I'm going to fall from a great height, and the drop will likely be fatal. There is sadness, fear, my entire body gone rigid with a final panicked intake of breath as if air can save me. And it does. I plummet in slow motion, in dips and waves like a revolving feather. Again my thoughts are faster than movement; my mind relaxes, thinking, "I'm rescued! Today I will not die." I land on the ground, on shining hardwood floors that receive me like a mattress. I'm standing, shaken but alive, unhurt. I look up at the ladder in wonder and thank the invisible ones who decided this was not the way I would leave this world.

The Courage to Hold Together

It's the summer of 2003 and a heartbreaking loss has resurrected Depression from inner depths. He's never left me, but sometimes I forget he's there, stretched out across my baseline. Devastated, I lose the ground beneath my feet, weeping melts the floor. There is only terrible falling. The elevator inside me drops and drops until I beg for the crash.

I'm tired of business as usual, tired of pulling myself back from the abyss. Sober, I know I'll cry myself to sleep and wake in the morning punched full of holes. I can't stand another breakfast of sorrow. So this time I egg myself on, run out to the liquor store a block from my building, one I rarely frequent because they traffic mainly in hard stuff rather than quality wines I sometimes enjoy. I buy a bottle of whiskey and proceed to drink my way to hysteria, to abandon. I tell myself I'd rather dance with death than despair. I drink my mind to the floor, where it sits, watching. Enraged heartbreak is running the show. It moves my body with cold efficiency and I stagger through the apartment, collecting what I need: a thick leather belt, the tall aluminum ladder. I drag the ladder beneath a hook pounded into a beam in my ceiling, meant for hanging a plant. I wear the belt on my neck, attach myself to the hook. I lean into the weight of my unhappiness. The ladder is cold. It holds me until I lose consciousness, then it falls away.

Hours later, lying horribly awake, exhausted but wired by medication, I realize the dream from a month earlier came true. I orchestrated a drop that should have been fatal but the invisible ones saved me. Perhaps it was ancestors who added their weight to mine, who wrapped the pain of their difficult stories around my legs and pulled, pulled, until the belt broke and plunged me to the floor. After which, I rise like a ghost, unnaturally calm. I straighten my dress, remove the toppled ladder to the back storage room. I wash my face and comb my hair, wipe away the blood on my neck.

When police show up for a wellness check, alerted by a concerned friend, my world appears ordered. The two men ask if I'm suicidal. The question slows time. I know they want nothing more than to turn around and continue their patrol, leave me to my business.

I look fine. I could easily lie and fool them. But an inner voice tells me that I need help, I can't go on this way. Depression is winning, claiming more of me each year. I take a breath and make the choice. I tell the truth.

What I come to realize is that in earlier years I would have lied. When you are held together with string, you work very hard to pretend that you are solid, you are whole. Appearances are everything, because they're all you have. Once you begin to progress and harbor bold suspicions that perhaps your life truly does have value, you are building a floor beneath your feet, something sturdier, more honest, to stand upon. In 2003, I am finally strong enough to fall apart, strong enough to ask for more than tape and string and flimsy patches. I allow myself to be admitted to a hospital and spend three nights there, working hard to learn new ways of talking to myself, new ways of framing old problems. I am suicidal from 1973 to 2003, and never since.

I am four generations removed from the trauma of White Stone Hill, four generations beyond a campaign of genocide. When I scratch at the past to see where our troubles began, the difficult road starts there. My family has suffered from a variety of diseases: Tuberculosis, Diabetes, Parkinson's, Cancer, Schizophrenia, Depression, Anxiety, PTSD, names you can find in diagnostic manuals. But these are only symptoms of underlying conditions: Racism, Greed, Exploitation, Plunder, Manifest Destiny, the Indian Reorganization Act, Indian Removal, Termination, the Indian Relocation Act, Colonization. Four generations later, my cousins and I still carry these plagues in our systems, these dark acts of betrayal and murder, these awful stories.

Our ancestors were taught to be strong, to keep moving forward one careful step at a time. They were taught to survive. So they crawled away from a massacre ground and rescued what few were still alive. They ate wild turnips. They never cried for themselves, or even for their children. Too many tears form a dangerous lake that can drown you. They passed on fortitude to the next generation, they passed on blood and breath and life, and the courage of survivors. They passed on grief and rage. My cousins and I sort through this complicated inheritance, seek to heal what was done to our ancestors. They cheer us on as we exhume what was buried, handle the dark matter and tissue. We look at everything that couldn't be examined in times of endless crisis. We hold our past as if it's a terrified child, we attend to its suffering. We are the generation that heals old wounds, not only to restore the health and stability our tribal nation once possessed, but also to give us strength and endurance to transform an ailing world.

Ancestors remind me that I am whole. That I come from a nation of extensive kinship networks that still bind us together across time. I come from a nation that values giving more than receiving, where the ones who are most revered are the ones who offer everything they have. They own nothing beyond their heart. I come from a nation in balance with territory and its many beings, where we honor sacred contracts with land and water, with muskrat, magpie, and the humblest wild onion. Ancestors tell me that what ails the generations beyond White Stone Hill, the military forts and reservations, the Indian boarding schools, is a borrowed sickness. It is not our true inheritance.

LONG LIVE THE FATHERLESS CHILDREN

Anika Fajardo

I let my father do the talking as we sat in the Colombian consul's spare office, eleven floors above the streets of San Francisco. Although Chicago is the closest Colombian consulate to my home in Minneapolis, the occasion of my brother's wedding in the Bay Area had provided the serendipity to visit San Francisco with my father.

"This is my daughter," he said in Spanish. He pulled out his ID card—his cédula—and showed it to the woman. My father's cédula was worn, the dog-eared corners proving his age, his longevity, the many years he had lived his life without me. If all went well today, I would be getting a cédula of my own in six months, a laminated card that proved I was my father's—and fatherland's—child.

"Bueno, señor," said the young woman, using the most polite version of Spanish I had ever heard, the language reserved for esteemed gentlemen, those whom younger people respectfully call "Don." My father had neat, gray, close-cut hair and the dignified posture of a man in his late seventies. His gray mustache was bushier than it was when I first met him twenty years ago, and it gave him a professorial look. I could have sworn I saw the consul bat her eyelashes for a split second.

While the woman went to photocopy his cédula, my father reviewed the diagram she had showed us that illustrated who was eligible for citizenship. The simplified drawing depicted a sort of family tree made up of disembodied heads. Two smiling faces, a man and a woman, for parents; one cherubic-faced child; an outline of the country of Colombia. If one parent is Colombian, the child is Colombian. Not only did I have one Colombian parent, I was also born in Colombia. So the facts seemed, at first, as simple as that diagram. Yet if I were to diagram my own family tree, how would I depict the American mother from Minnesota and the absent Colombian father, the birthplace, the lifelong residency? Facts and studies, rules and research all seem immutable and yet can be malleable, frequently succumbing to exceptions.

"Con permiso," the consul said when she returned. She explained in Spanish, mostly to my father, that we needed to get passport photos of me, stamps so that the passport could be mailed to me, and a cashier's check to pay for the fees. A scavenger hunt. We could do all of this now at the businesses on Market Street, she told us.

On the ground floor, we took a right turn out of the office building and found the Walgreens where the consul said we would. A handful of customers strolled the shop's two aisles. My father and I were just two more people wandering among the cereal boxes and Band-Aids, the Post-its and nail clippers.

"Is this where she said we can get your photo taken?" my father asked in his thick accent. Although my parents had lived in Minnesota for a year or so before I was born, he hadn't been back in the United States in more than forty years. He spotted a worker in a red vest. "Sir," he said, "do you have photos?"

The man, younger than my father but older than I, looked at us. "What are you looking for?" The man was brown skinned but not as dark as my father.

"I need passport photos," I said. This time my father let me do the talking. "And stamps," I added. "Can we get a cashier's check here?"

The man told us he could do the pictures and the stamps but that we would need to go somewhere else for the cashier's check. I wondered how many families this man saw that had been sent on errands by the Colombian consulate. How many fathers and daughters had he seen? Could he tell that we were different? Because, of course, we all believe we are different. "And you have to pay cash," he said. "The credit card reader is broken."

My wallet might have had a couple of twenties, but I functioned with my Visa card. I turned to my father. "Do you have cash?"

"I will pay," he said. He pulled a wad of dollars out of his pocket. Colombian pesos are almost all paper bills—some probably worth less than the paper they're printed on—and the U.S. dollars must have felt like play money to him. Even though he didn't seem to realize it, he held a lot of money in his hands and I wanted to tell him to put it away. Just because something looks familiar doesn't mean you understand it.

He turned to the man. "I am paying," he said.

When my parents got divorced in 1976—ahead of the sharply inclining curve of divorces in the United States—my father hadn't paid. The judge in Minnesota had ordered him to pay one hundred dollars—an amount equivalent to almost five hundred dollars today—but he never paid the judge's fee and he never paid child support. He returned to Colombia and it had been as if he had never existed.

It was fairly uncommon to be fatherless when I was a child in the 1980s. The middle-class white families of my neighborhood tended to have both parents, more than one child, and split-level ranch houses. I remember seeing my white friends' dads come home from work, surly or silent. They plopped into recliners or dining chairs. Those stoic, Minnesotan men rarely spoke, and when they did, their conversations were about lawn mowing and auto mechanics. Those were the times when I didn't care that I didn't have a dad. But sometimes, during a sleepover, a father would sit on the floor among the sleeping bags and giggling girls and tell ghost stories. Sometimes a friend's father would bring home a box of ice cream sandwiches and let us eat them on the front step before dinner. Sometimes someone else's dad would sneak a kiss on the nape of a mother's neck.

Today, according to government statistics, an estimated one in three children live without their biological fathers (due, so they say, to an increase of unwed mothers and rates of divorce), and about 40 percent of Hispanic children have single parents—more than average, less than Black and Native American children. Psychologists blame all kinds of ills on the absent father. Fatherless children are more likely to be incarcerated. More likely to have teen pregnancies. More likely to live in poverty. More likely to drop out of high school. More likely to commit suicide. Those are the facts, the studies. Facts that I want to dismiss as too stereotyping, too monolithic. And yet I depend on facts to prove me to be the exception, different: I have an advanced degree and had a child well within the confines of wedlock. And I've never even had a speeding ticket.

After the passport photos were taken, my father and I headed down Market Street in search of the cashier's check. The sun had broken through San Francisco's fog and we squinted in the heat. Around us, workers in the financial district were trickling out for their lunch breaks, clogging the sidewalks. The throngs made my father seem even smaller and grayer. How much had changed in the United States since my father was last in this country? He grabbed my hand, almost as if he were protecting me in the crowds, but the gesture was more of a comfort to him than me.

First we stopped in a bank's lobby. I remembered queueing in a bank line when I first visited my father at the age of twenty-one. Colombia was so foreign then, in the 1990s, when everything was less connected. Now the bank receptionist told us we couldn't get a cashier's check unless we were customers. Rules and regulations. She looked at me and I shook my head. My father reached into his pocket for his cash and opened his mouth as if to protest or haggle; regulations are sometimes easier to circumvent in Colombia. I pulled him away. "Try the 7-Eleven," the receptionist called after us.

I led my father across the street, down the block. I hadn't been in a 7-Eleven since I was a kid in Minnesota. On those evenings when my mom went on dates or out with her girlfriends, my babysitter bought me candy from the 7-Eleven near the apartment complex where we lived. Time and distance haven't changed the convenience store much—this one still had the same plasticky smell that I remember, the same flicking overhead lights, the same customers desperate for Mountain Dew and Camel Lights and scratch-off tickets. While we stood in line, my father again pulled the bills from his pocket, sorting through the twenties and fives. I wanted to reprimand him, to tell him not to flash his wad of cash around. But I was the child. Wasn't I? How do we transition from child to adult in the eyes of our parents? Especially in those who've been absent?

Those researchers of academic studies will tell you the repercussions of missing fathers, the generational impact of not having two parents. They say that sons of absent fathers are more likely to be absent in their own children's lives (and yet my half-brother, who experienced as much if not more of the impacts of our father's absence, lives with, parents, and provides for his wife and two children) and that daughters of absent fathers are more likely to have children with men who themselves will be absent (and yet I am celebrating my twentieth wedding anniversary with the father of my own daughter).

While paying for the cashier's check, my father placed a bottle of Coca-Cola on the counter. "I'm hungry," he said. "Aren't you hungry?" I thought of the lunchtime crowds and the wait we still had ahead of us at the consulate and nodded. As we made our way back to the office, we passed the bottle of Coke back and forth. When I visited him that first time when I was twenty-one, I had been insulted that he didn't seem to think I was old enough to join him for a beer. Do daughters ever grow up in the eyes of their fathers? At the time, he thought of me as his child and gave me Coke while he sipped his Club Colombia beer.

Back at the consulate, my father and I sat down again to wait our turn. One by one, the other families in the waiting room were called up, their business executed. I watched these Colombians who lived in the United States. I had never seen so many Colombians outside of Colombia. What business did they have? I wondered. There was an older couple huddled together; two young women; a few single men silent, alone. They had brown faces and pale faces. Dark hair like mine, like my father's was before the grays took over. Could they tell that I was his daughter? Could they guess that I was not—yet—a Colombian citizen?

Soon my father and I were the only ones left in the waiting room. He passed me the bottle of Coke. Before my parents separated, before they were divorced, before I grew up without a father in Minnesota, they were married and raising a baby together. My father cared for me while my mother was at her job teaching English. If you research absent Hispanic fathers like I did, you find hundreds of academic articles with words like *crime* and *disadvantages, abuse* and *abandonment, incarceration* and *morbidity* in their titles. They paint a picture of deprived children and neglectful men. Where is the picture of a father holding a chubby baby on his lap, bringing a bottle of warm milk to her lips?

When the consul called my name, my father tightly screwed the cap on the Coca-Cola. We arrived at the desk armed with all the spoils of the hunt: the stamps, the photos, the check. The woman jotted down notes, typed on a computer, and explained things. I nodded, but I let my father do the talking. He took over, explaining again the situation of my birth, my Americanness, my lack of fluent Spanish. All the facts. He asked questions, read off his cédula number. The woman asked me something and then looked at me like I was a child when I couldn't answer. This time it felt like I was the one flashing a wad of cash around San Francisco.

"It's done," he said at last, grinning. I was now—officially—a Colombian citizen. And yet still American. I would hold dual citizenship, an official split between two countries, with the documentation to prove it. The paperwork also seemed like proof that I was my father's daughter. I had always been his daughter, of course, but whether we are raised with our parents or separated from them, our relationships with them are constantly shifting, moving, changing. Even the facts can't tell the whole story because they don't consider the multiple truths we hold. My father missed his children's upbringing and yet now he would witness his son's wedding and play with his grandchildren. My father was absent for my childhood and yet here he was, smiling at me in the consul's office.

The woman handed me a paper ID card with my photo on it. I have a surprised, bemused look on my face as if I can't quite believe I'm at a Walgreens in San Francisco with my father being photographed for a Colombian passport. Even though the picture was taken just a few hours earlier, the woman on the temporary cédula already seems like an alternate version of myself.

"You are a Colombian citizen." He hugged me. Perhaps my father, too, was an alternate version. We all are, aren't we? I am not the same baby being fed warm milk, I am not the same child cared for by her single mother, and I am not even the same woman who walked into the Colombian consulate a few hours earlier. We are more than we seem, more than the world would have us be. My father is more than an absent father, more than a divorced Colombian man, more than a parent who didn't get to know his children until they were adults. "Congratulations."

"Viva Colombia," I said, laughing, and let my father take my hand in his as we walked to the elevator.

LAND ACKNOWLEDGMENT STATEMENT OF A NATIVE VIRGINIAN

Mary Moore Easter

The land I grew up on
was owned by white people
before Daddy and Mama bought four acres
one mile past the railroad tracks
—country, not city.
Not a good deal for us black folks, they thought
squirreling our borrowed cash
into their overall pockets.
Too swampy, too low to farm.
Never our aim anyway.
Rain would collect in grass puddles
as if the county drained downhill
to our "land of a thousand lakes," Mama joked,
when faraway Minnesota only gave us a tag line
without Dakota, Ojibwe, and Lakota.
So intense was the way color cleaved our world
into black and white, that thoughts of original life
on the land were chopped into small bits and
buried the way conquerors do everywhere.

Whose land did I grow up on?
Ours, I blurt. Ours
from the age of eleven when bulldozers
first broke ground and workmen tied strings to wooden stakes
to show the rooms to come.
Taken there by car—
it was country, we thought,
a whole mile from the railroad
at the edge of town—
taken there to understand ownership with my body,
I walked the muddy ruts
and stood inside the strings that marked my room,
the space that would hold my bed and bedside table
under a bank of windows,
glass that opened out like a clam's shell,
the room where a polished wood plinth
would stretch above desk drawer and chest of drawers,
to the vanity before the doorway.
Who could imagine all that would fit
on this square of string-marked mud?

From the moment of my eleven-year-old visit
through each construction trip to see brick on brick ascend,
brush cleared, land drained, it was ours,
open space uncrowded by the latest racial restrictions,
ours, outside that web thick with honeysuckle parasite,
sweet southern ooze, and killing vine.

Here in the piedmont of Virginia, south of the James River
no one talked of the people, Algonquian, and Appomattocs
even though we knew the name of the river that flowed
through town when we went into the city
and the Battle of Appomattox in the Civil War.

Who could make me know that any but white people—
Brits, Scots—had held it before us?

And which white people acknowledged the land
belonged to others before they took it in the name of the king?
Yes, that far back, before America was America.
Our four acres was a parcel in Southside
in what would become the Commonwealth of Virginia,
not Tidewater to the east or Blue Ridge to the west,
not Potomac to the north but Southside
from the James River down to the North Carolina line.

We knew black land, enslaved, free, and covenanted against,
we knew the British, who made every parish royal
King William, Prince Edward, Prince George,
but no one talked of Cherokee, Cheroakan,
Chickahominy, Matoacan, Monacan.
Matoaca gave its name to my elementary school
(*Indian,* they nodded), then skipped to Pocahontas,
royalty famed by her marriage to John Smith.
Pamunkey Indians were nowhere
in our knowledge, never connected to their Princess Matoaka
whom we only knew by her Pocahontas nickname.
Not that they mastered the flow and puddle,
and the corn thriving just beyond our back fence line.

Nothing of Meherrin, Nottoway,
Paleo, Powhatan (yes, we knew Powhatan),
Roanoke, Saponi, Weyanoke,
and all their relatives
who lived there among my roots
claimed the flats and grasses
some for seasonal passing
others to own sand and rivers.
And the victors, to wrench turf by the root hairs
from those who came before.
I call their names.

FINANCIAL TRAUMA

Tess Montgomery

Have you ever woken up from sleep on payday and felt anxiety as you reached for your phone to open the bank app to check your balance? As you wait for your fingerprint on the phone to be identified, you run through in your head every bill that needs to be paid while you nervously await the verdict: "How much will my paycheck cover?"

I grew up in a low-income, single-parent household. My mother worked full-time, but we did not have discretionary money for anything. The only reason to check the mail was in anticipation of her paycheck. Otherwise it was bills and junk mail. *Broke* was a term I learned early.

As I have grown into adulthood, I realize I have never had what many would consider a healthy relationship with money. In talking with friends who are women of color like me, I have discovered that many of them have similar issues. I began to wonder if there might be something to learn there and set out to discover what that might be.

What I found is that for many of us, there is trauma associated with finances—trauma that has been carried through many generations.

We talk about the effects of historical trauma related to oppression and being marginalized. The intense emotions that come with financial struggles, however, are rarely mentioned. The shame, the guilt, the feeling of being gaslighted by your own bank account, memory loss over spending, paranoia that you were overcharged, and mistrust that you are underpaid are all part of the constant stress about money for so many women.

Women have increasingly become the sole provider for our households. We have obtained the highest rates of education and are progressively landing more management and leadership positions. Even in cases where men are a main household provider, women still play a vital role in making key decisions about how the money is spent.

However, there have been fierce and sudden changes in family structure caused by a history of patriarchy and white supremacy. Men continue to be torn from their families—lynched, imprisoned, and deported—leaving women to deal with the aftermath. Most women have never been taught to be confident with money. There are so many unconscious ideas embedded in our relationship to money, generally tied to our sense of worth and value, and associated with crisis. Financial trauma is pervasive, yet largely unaddressed.

A study on disparities from Minnesota Compass indicates that people of color are more likely to live in poverty, less likely to own a home, and tend to stop short on educational goals. Although disparities are rooted in historical experiences of oppression and exclusion, data show that gaps can be explained by insufficient income, unhealthy environments, and inadequate access to opportunities. The report concludes: "We can address all of these."

Poverty is one of the legacies of historical trauma. Many white communities have accumulated wealth that gets passed down. In communities of color, however, we often need to help our parents pay bills at an early age, and education is disrupted by having to help out with childcare for our younger siblings, and with cooking and cleaning while our parents struggle to earn a living. If you are from an immigrant family, you are often responsible for helping family members both here and abroad.

I have been involved in the More Than a Single Story discussions where women from a variety of communities of color have talked about the ways these practices have been woven throughout their lives. "You see your parents paying the bills, but no one tells you why the lights got turned off." "My grandparents didn't believe in banks, so we would hide money around the house."

One panelist quoted poet Nayyirah Waheed: "All the women in me are tired." She added later, "Women have to run a marathon just to get to the starting line."

Nods of familiarity and deep exhales from audience members filled the room.

Through self-assessment and the help of community and culturally minded organizations like the Black Women's Wealth Alliance or WomenVenture, I have learned that we women can learn ways to break generational patterns of loss, scarcity, and poverty. Current technology offers assistance in creating a system of control. Apps like Mint, Credit Karma, and Digit help to track spending, credit scores, and savings.

It is a constant battle for women to find the time and energy to raise children, and themselves, while meeting the demands of working for an income that allows us to survive. No one talks about how expensive it is to be poor.

Managing with Not Much of Anything

For months now, news stories have been consumed with the threats of Covid-19 and the effect this pandemic will have on the stock market, and U.S. and global economies.

When I see these articles, I can't help but think, "What's that got to do with me?" The closest thing I have to a stock is made with beef or chicken.

I don't know if I am lucky or not so lucky to have no worries about my investments or retirement funds. How can I, when I am only thinking about how I am going to make it through another week?

Like many others, I watched cautiously as the threat of Covid-19 grew closer and swarms of people rushed to the grocery store to "prepare-not-panic" shop. What do you do when a pandemic hits between paychecks? How do you manage being caught up in the hustle of feeling pressured to be prepared but being financially limited? Suddenly, you are faced with decisions like whether you should buy cleaning wipes—if you can find them—or another pack of chicken breasts.

Mothers are faced with the question of how they are going to feed their children three meals every day of the week—while attempting to work from home, not getting paid at all, or being required to go off to work with kids at home.

We quickly saw how a crisis can turn into class warfare. Those with privilege hoarded essential supplies because they had the money to do so.

I do see a silver lining in times like this, however. You see the humanity in poverty.

Unfortunately, for women of color, we have practiced for this. It isn't new to us. Relying on community support is how we survive even when there is not a pandemic. Food drives, granny day care, cash advances from close friends and family are all part of the poor person's savings account.

As I have learned from More Than a Single Story conversations, communities of color are resilient. We are adaptable. As my mother used to say, "We will get through this, just like all the other times."

And What about Reparations?

Growing up, I always heard of reparations being financial, like a monetary check being sent to descendants of slavery or a Holocaust, or to Native Americans. But now, especially thinking of financial trauma in our community, and seeing that unfold in various ways, I wonder if a one-time check would be enough or even smart—to hand a large sum of money to people who have never received that amount of money before.

While there is some validity to saying that people are in control of their own lives, we also know what financial trauma can play out to be—materialistic spending, compensatory consumption. I mean, you're trying to compensate for all the years of not having money so now you're gonna go out and buy TVs and Jordans and what have you, instead of investing and saving and watching it build. People who haven't had anything often do not understand the value of watching it build. We don't even know what that means.

Speaking for myself, I'm just now learning what it's like to build a savings account from five dollars to five hundred dollars or whatever, and to see what comes of that. So when I think of the background of financial trauma in our communities, I'm beginning to agree more and more with people who are talking about reparations being free medical and mental healthcare, free access to education and higher education opportunities, instead of handing out money. Maybe even handing out houses.

But along with that, there needs to be massive education on the effects of financial trauma as a huge part of the traumas we've experienced for 401 years and how we can turn those effects around as individuals and families. That kind of education along with training in financial management and investing would go much further than just handing out a check.

CROSS POLLINATION

Kathryn Haddad

The zucchini seeds were wrapped in a small piece of paper and taped up tightly like a little present. I don't remember the exchange before getting them, but I must have mentioned something about liking *koosa*—the Arabic word for the vegetable—and the next week in the church aisle after the service, the old man pulled a package out of the pocket of his suit coat in that slow, methodical way that old people do things. His hands were smooth, firm, and strong. They reminded me of my father's. "For you," he said, and put them in my palm like a treasure. "Seeds from Lebanon."

He had been a friend of my father, and I had heard his name before, but I didn't meet him until after my father died and I started to go to church every week with my mom to provide her some of the familiarity of her former life. But I was quickly drawn in by the beauty of the Arabic and Aramaic chanting and singing, and by the philosophical lessons, the poetry of the ceremony, and the stories. It felt good to be around the old people that my dad knew in this American space.

I am Lebanese. American. Lebanese American. My father was born in Lebanon. My mother's family were immigrants from Europe more than a century ago. I am the result of cross pollination.

I thanked the old man, as he gently grasped my hands with his for a minute and let go, and wondered about this treasure from the "old country." Seeds from Lebanon! I was touched by this small gift.

I brought the package home and put it in my cupboard intending to plant them later that spring. But for some reason I didn't do it that year. As spring turned to summer, and the gardens started to take off, the old man asked me about them. He wondered if I had put them in the ground. Did they grow? Yes! I planted them! Thank you! They are growing very well! But I did not plant them. Throughout that entire summer he asked me how they were doing, and since I had started the lie, I had to keep it up. I invented a fake zucchini crop. "They are growing great! So big! Lots of koosa! Delicious. Thanks again!" I would say and hurry away. I was relieved when fall and then winter came, and the questions stopped.

This year as the pandemic orders came to stay indoors, I was searching through the cupboard for things to do, and I remembered the little package of seeds. As I pulled off the tape from the tightly wrapped paper he had given me and finally actually looked at them, I was surprised to find they were smaller than any zucchini seeds I had seen before. They were also painted a weird bright green color. Maybe I misunderstood what he had said to me or he had misunderstood what I had said to him. Is that why he kept asking me about the garden? I was embarrassed remembering our conversations.

When I finally planted the seeds, I had very little expectation that they would even grow at all. So I was surprised when they immediately started to sprout. I took a picture of them and entered it into my PictureThis plant app. It identified them as pumpkin. I had no room for a bunch of pumpkin plants! And I was hoping for a big meal of koosa.

Now, I am no gardener, really. I have a small piece of dirt in the backyard that I hack away at. The soil is rough and old with little nutrients, and weeds and creeping Charlie take root and usually strangle things out. But the one thing I do like to grow, and the one thing that does grow is zucchini.

Lebanese zucchini is unique, because they are a different variety from what you can find around here. They are roundish and lighter green, and perfect for hollowing out and stuffing with meat and rice—a delicacy that I savor from my childhood. The zucchini that you find in Minnesota are dark green and long—difficult for coring and stuffing. In actuality, growing up in Minnesota, I really never even saw the round ones, only in pictures. Every fall on Labor Day weekend, my father would get a bunch of zucchini from Rainbow Foods, and we would spend the day struggling to core and stuff them because of their size. We would invite my mother's brother and wife over to have an end-of-summer koosa party. This party stopped when my uncle died. And then the coring and stuffing finally stopped when my father died, and we sold the house.

Well, the plant app was wrong. They were zucchini! As they grew, they also appeared to be the roundish, light green ones from Lebanon that are perfect for stuffing. The old man was honest in the end, and I felt really bad for all of my suspicious thoughts and embarrassment in potential misunderstandings from a few years back.

I can't tell him this year about the zucchini that grew from his seeds because I haven't seen him, or any of the Lebanese people that I got to know at the church since my dad died because of the Covid-19 restrictions, and my fears of going into crowded places and infecting my mother.

So as these zucchini took off, I decided to let one of the vegetables get really huge in order to have my own seeds for the future. And one of the vegetables grew and grew and grew. It grew so big that it was almost like something I could have entered in the state fair for a contest, if we had the fair this year. Finally, I picked it because I was a little scared of its bloated size, and I was excited to gather the seeds.

I took the large vegetable into the house, cut it open, and hundreds of seeds were perfect inside! It was exciting to think about how many zucchini I could have in the future.

My mother helped me sort the small insignificant seeds from the large ones that I hoped would reproduce. She is staying with me this week. Since my father died, she has been living between an assisted care facility, my sister's house, and mine. It isn't easy.

I probably got about three hundred seeds from the big zucchini. I laid them out on a cookie sheet on some wax paper on top of the stove, drying under the light, and when I got nervous, I would go over to them where they were drying and turn them over. It was calming to touch the seeds, to look at them, to imagine what they could become.

My mother told me that it would be impossible to grow three hundred zucchini plants in my small plot in the back of my yard in my lifetime, even if I did freeze all of the seeds and save them for however long they would save. She told me to throw the extras away, but I could not do that. I started to think that maybe I could supply all of the lost Lebanese American children like myself with these seeds! I would quite literally seed the land with our heritage vegetable, and every Arab American looking for a connection to their past could find it in their backyard. It would be my little contribution to heal the wounds of all those times we were longing for our food and culture. I could help bring Lebanon to Minnesota.

As my plans got bigger for the seeds, I started to dream about my connection to this ancient plant and my ancestors. I imagined my great-great-great-grandmother harvesting zucchini in the mountains, and the village gathering for feasts. For thousands of years, my people had been eating it at family feasts, and here I was continuing on with the tradition!

I decided to do a little research on the zucchini.

I looked up the etymology of the word and found that the Arabic word *koosa* كوسة was actually the name given to the vegetable quite recently because it looked like a cucumber (which has a very similar name). In fact, further research told me that the zucchini didn't even appear in Lebanon until perhaps the early twentieth century—most likely from travelers. I had to read it several times. It isn't Lebanese at all. The koosa in Lebanon is a settler. An immigrant. A squatter.

And then I remembered my lessons from elementary school. Squash was one of the primary foods of the First Nations people of the Americas. How did I forget? Zucchini is native to the Americas!

And the package the old man gifted me was on its trip back home to the Midwest where it originated.

It's like me. A hybrid. A cross between here and there.

I am thinking that next spring I will continue with my plan to put the seeds from the zucchini the old man gave me in little paper packages and mail them off to my lost Arab American community. But this time, I will do it with a feeling of appreciation of the land I live on and a message of welcome home.

BREATH

A Meditation in Uprising

Erin Sharkey

A smoky haze snaked in our window air conditioning unit and pooled around our ceiling. After seventy-five days of sheltering in place to avoid Covid-19, my partner, Zoe, and I packed essential paperwork, medicine, and a few keepsakes and left our block in South Minneapolis to sleep at my parents' home in a northern suburb of the Twin Cities. Up until then, it had been my lungs that kept us holed up inside our six-hundred-square-foot apartment, aside from two short walks a day with our geriatric boxer, Lucy. For weeks groceries, take-out meals, and prescriptions were delivered to the front door of our condo building, with no contact.

We had been staying away from my parents and the rest of our family because my parents were part of high-risk groups and my brothers were essential workers. I have had asthma my whole life and it was the primary reason we had been isolating. First, there was heightened fear of contracting coronavirus myself because of the ways asthma and its inflammation can compromise the immune system; and second, there was fear of passing it along to the people I care about most. I have risk factors in addition to my lungs and my health history: my size (fat), and my racial identity (mixed-race

Black). I was not confident I would receive the necessary care if I were to get sick.

The day we woke up to a smoke-filled apartment was the third morning after the police killed George Floyd, kneeled on his neck for more than nine minutes. Just blocks from our home, they asphyxiated him, his face ground into the black concrete of the street, on camera, in front of witnesses. People from all over the world saw the video and witnessed our disgust and anger boil over and burst into flames.

Zoe and I stayed at my parents' house for three nights, awake in the flickering blue light of television, watching our neighborhood burn on CNN. My mother and my (step)father sat in their retirement positions in two matching recliners, mom with her legs crossed at the ankles, dad with his arms crossed at his chest, and called out locations they recognized from the live news feed. A stack of Bible study texts, a folded TV schedule from the newspaper, and a pile of remotes sat on the table between them. On the second night, after a news story about members of the Minneapolis City Council's adoption of commitment to defund the MPD, my dad and I discussed our opinions of abolition. Our voices climbed in competition, each of us shocked at the other's stance. My mom tried to soothe what she perceived as a conflict between us, but I was thrilled for the opportunity to test the strength of my thinking and to poke holes in his logic. My dad, the man my mom married before I was in kindergarten, is a very smart man who processes information very differently from the way I do. I wanted to see the idea bounce around inside him, knocking against his deep commitment to his faith, his experience as a bureaucrat, and his particular brand of pessimism, as well as his identities as a white man born in the Baby Boom generation.

After three nights, concern for our neighborhood and our work as organizers called us home. That was a month ago.

I wake up tight, a rubber band wrapped around my lungs. Do I have Covid-19? Is this how it starts? Maybe I got it running errands yesterday. But the symptoms probably wouldn't present that quickly. We have started to venture out a little more, but I am always careful and stay in the car, using curbside pickup and drive-through options. I inventory all my precautions and try to start my day.

I think of all the people who don't wear masks and I think about Covid-19 again. Maybe I contracted the virus from a casual encounter, taking out the trash, getting the mail, opening the mail, greeting a neighbor from six feet (maybe it was four feet) while walking my dog. Maybe I got it from a doorknob or the railing down the five steps to the front door from our first-floor apartment. I remind myself I am cautious and try not to touch anything between our door and the open air.

My lungs tighten. Not yet an attack. A sinking suspicion, a hint that something might be coming. A storm darkening in the sky off by the horizon.

Maybe it is just the weather? Or seasonal allergies? It has been raining for days. Loud thunder has broken our sleep for the past few nights. The days have been warming and humid—that can make me wheeze because changes in barometric pressure can affect my breathing. My mom used to say my lungs broadcast a pretty accurate forecast. A storm brews inside me long before thunder and lightning crack across the sky. I take my white inhaler. It clicks open with the sound of powder breaking free of its little compartment. I suck it into my lungs and hold it there. The fine dust doesn't feel or taste like anything. I have to trust that the medicine is being pulled in to do its work. The white inhaler has a steroid in it that helps prevent asthma attacks. I won't feel this one working for hours.

I take my blue inhaler. This one is a rescue inhaler, like others I have taken for almost forty years. When I was younger, it was a creamsicle color. For a while, it was red. Oh, and I think there was a time it was gray with a red cap. To operate this inhaler, I plunge it in from the top and suck the mist. The timing is like double Dutch; pull too early (or too late) and the spray hits my tongue or the back of my throat. This time I catch a cloud on the wind; I carry it to the tree-like system in my lungs.

The medicine and my brain work to order the disquiet of my anxious thinking, begin to diminish the tension.

My wife and I haven't done much socializing. By distance, we have seen my parents and my brother and his wife and my little nephews, watched from across the yard as the kids played. Some friends have come by to stand or set up a lawn chair under our front window. We spend time together that way. I celebrated my best friend's nomination for a Minnesota Book Award, separated from her by a sheet of glass on her front porch. In addition to hours and hours a day in Zoom rooms, we have (re)connected with friends who live far away via video conferencing. We share no embraces, no food from the same plate, no sips of each other's drinks. We don't share smells or textures.

It took days to consider whether I would protest George Floyd's murder outside with other protesters. We volunteered to use our car and drove in the middle of the march to help with pacing and supplies. We balanced the fear of Covid-19 and the strength of our moral rousing because we needed to be with our people. On all sides, as far as I could see in front of our car and as far as I could see in the rearview mirror, were our people on foot and pushing bikes beside them, with handmade signs and T-shirts, yelling and chanting and together.

My lungs order from the whole menu of asthma triggers. Allergies: pet dander, dust, pollen, mold, freshly cut grass, new car smell. I wheeze when I get sunburned. Odors like cigarette smoke, campfires, smog, strong perfume, cleaning chemicals, fuel (especially diesel). I have exercise-induced asthma. Weather changes are a trigger. My emotions and hormones. When I was an adolescent, during the months after I started menstruation, I would end up in the ER on the first day of my cycle. My lungs constrict when I am sad or excited, angry, scared, nervous.

I have seen the heart of my city broken before. On a Sunday morning in November 2015, we found ourselves—my friends and my partner and me—on a street corner in North Minneapolis, listening to the accounts of community members who had witnessed the police kill a young unarmed Black man in the yellow glow of a streetlight on a cold fall night near midnight.

The sky was bright on that Sunday morning, and the air had an orange tint and the sun burnt warm and long. Out of the testimony of neighbors grew a protest that marched down Plymouth Avenue to the city's fourth police precinct. People took up camp there, and we chanted Jamar Clark's name and raised our fists, demanding that the police release the video of the killing and demanding justice for his murder. When the mainstream media reported from the scene, in the picture they painted, we protesters shrunk in membership; we were angry grotesque masks; we seemed gnarled and irrational. Our rightful, mournful anger was transcribed as violent. Our peaceful co-ordination was portrayed as stumbling and visionless.

That wasn't the only time we took to the streets. Not even a year later, after the murder of Philando Castile, we rang the governor's doorbell in the middle of the night and demanded that the state wake up and answer for another killing by police. We took over the street there for days.

This time fires raged at the city's third precinct, and the anger and the flames moved down Lake Street to our home. We live in the Powderhorn Park neighborhood, an enclave known for hippies and radicals that surrounds a park named before the Civil War, for the little lake at the center that is shaped like a horn to hold gun powder. My partner and I live on the park's northern edge.

When the neighborhood was ablaze, the police and National Guard set up shop on our corner with their vehicles and bright lights. Our neighbors worked together under threat of White Nationalists and other malevolent outsiders determined to enact a purge born of some cinematic fantasy.

Sometimes during quiet moments with others, I am self-conscious because my body isn't quiet. When everyone around me is still and soft, like in prayer or meditation, my breath rattles out of me, loud and grating.

I have had asthma since I came into this world. As an infant, I had wet, crackly breath, and patches of my brown skin went white because the eczema made me lose pigment in rough patches on my cheeks, chest, and arms. When I was a child, doctors would offer that some people grow out of their asthma. But I was scared to hope for that. Hoping felt like reaching for something too far away. I spent many nights under the fluorescent lights of an emergency room, my body stiff, my rigid arms holding up my upper body.

I have grown some distance from the disease. My asthma used to be more severe and chronic, but it has waned a bit as I've gotten older. Or I have learned to better control it with more responsible attention to care. Though it no longer requires daily maintenance, nor have I been hospitalized in many years, asthma is still there waiting at the margins of my life. That is why the little whispers of wheezing are haunting, like a ghost I have started to forget making the floorboards creak in a room down the hall.

The months leading up to my thirty-fifth birthday, the fall of 2015, were stressful and thrilling. I was balancing graduate school and work alongside other Black organizers in response to the killing of Jamar Clark. One night, at the encampment that grew around the fourth precinct building on the city's north side, after days and days of protesting, the smoke got really thick. There were bonfires in the street because night was coming on earlier each day and the fall had begun to chill the air. That night, the police used tear gas or some other irritant to convince us protesters to go home, and my lungs started constricting and a little cough turned into many in a chain. I could feel my lungs tighten. I heard the strain in my exhaled breath.

A Black artist friend appeared through the smoke with a mask for me to wear. It helped me breathe.

The ripple effect of that time has moved through many friendships, as has unattended trauma.

We are wearing masks all the time now.

Some describe an asthma attack as feeling like an elephant is sitting on your chest. Like you can't get air in and you can't get air out. I haven't watched the whole video. Can't bring myself to watch George Floyd's life extinguished. Don't need to. I saw enough to see the life being smashed out of him. I have been inside a body fighting for breath, fighting to live. Kicking for breath. Resisting death. But nothing I experienced is like the violence of an evil agent of an evil state sitting on my chest. George Floyd died with the weight of the state ground into him.

Nine minutes and twenty-nine seconds is a horribly long time to drown in cacophony.

Ben Crump, the attorney for George Floyd's family, while talking about the results of the Hennepin County medical examiner's report on Floyd's death, which indicated that he had had Covid-19 as well as asthma, said, "We saw in the Eric Garner case . . . . [George Floyd] had asthma, he had a heart condition—all these things that are irrelevant when they were living, breathing, walking, talking, just fine until the police accosted them."

I have always been a social person, but asthma has affected my ability to trust others. While my friends got to be reckless, losing their inhibitions and control, I had to remain vigilant. I don't smoke or drink. As a teenager, I learned alcohol triggers my asthma—makes my lungs tight and wheezy and my face flush and sweaty. Throughout my teens and twenties, this made me the constant sober driver. I have never smoked a cigarette, because just visiting the home of a smoker or going to a smoky restaurant or bar has landed me in the hospital.

There was a Thanksgiving dinner in the street outside the Fourth Precinct in the fall of 2015. I completed my MFA that fall, and after my final reading and celebration my family and friends brought my cake to the protest site, because many of my friends could not attend because they were protesting there. "Congratulations" was scripted in frosting across the top.

My birthday party a few weeks later was boycotted by friends who chose to not attend because white people would be in attendance. I understood and respected their boundary, though I have to admit it stung. Isolation is woven into my racial identity. As a mixed-race child in a white family, I had little community from which to learn or with which to commune around my Blackness. To hold identity as a mixed Black person can be challenging because in addition to the privilege that comes with whiteness, it also asks that you occupy an intimate position to its inherent violence. But to choose between them feels impossible.

The excitement of my birthday landed me in the ER more than once when I was a child. With neighborhood friends, kids from school, and my cousins chasing around the party, opening my throat in shrill glee, my heart would be racing and my little lungs overstimulated. I'm sure I ignored the roaring in my chest to stay inside the celebration a little bit longer. The evening would end up in an exam room with another nurse noticing my birthdate on my chart and asking why I chose this place to celebrate. I must have made a wrong turn somewhere.

Erin Sharkey

In Chinese medicine, the lungs hold grief. The Heart Chakra is associated with air, abandonment, rejection, and losing oneself in another. It glows green. Once many years ago, a woman hovered her open palms over my chest in a Reiki practice and asked if I was heartbroken. She speculated that my father had broken it. "Many people with asthma have hurt that comes from their fathers," she said.

You see, I have two fathers. One father, who was at that time, present, White and bald, and one father, absent, Black and tall, who had been gone for many years, since before I started kindergarten. I had, at that moment, one father who I liked to debate with. And I suspected the woman was asking about my absent father, so I told her I wasn't sure I knew him well enough to be heartbroken. My father's nickname is Big Curt, because he is so tall. We are no longer absent from one another. Now that I have gotten to know him, I would describe him as a gentle giant.

George Floyd was known as Big Floyd because of his height. At his memorial service, people who knew him described him as a gentle giant. He was a father to five.

DEAR EDITOR

Douglas Kearney

Scant days after Derek Chauvin murdered George Floyd, I received an email from an editor of an online magazine. The email was a request to respond to the murder, calling on—roughly—my expertise in antiblackness, my stature, and my proximity "on-the-ground" (an unfortunate choice of words) in the Twin Cities. Instead of producing an exclusive comment, I posted a version of this statement on my Facebook account on June 5, 2020. It was late in the morning. Almost noon.

I have made very few revisions. —D.K.

Dear Editor,

I thank you for this invitation. Funny, I composed a poem about the historic Watts uprisings on Sunday, May 24, before the MPD murdered George Floyd.

There's a part of me that wants to simply send you all of what I've already written. Not as some authority, but to point out simply that this is a changing same. That I—and many others—are always thinking about the conditions under which George Floyd and so many, many others are subject, the combination of these as features, not bugs, in systemic modes of violence that are a part of the purview of policing. As my wife and I explained to our ten-year-olds (who learned explicitly about a then-contemporaneous application of this constant, historic killing when St. Anthony police officer Jeronimo

Yanez murdered Philando Castile): it isn't that law enforcement is simply disinterested in protecting Black people, but that U.S. Culture/Law dictate that our very presence is the thing they are meant to protect against.

That white comfort has come to define itself as dependent on methodical control of *everyone* they deem "other" is true—settler colonialism, slavery, racism, forced displacement within the country, deportation, xenophobia, lynching, segregation, official exclusionary acts, internment, redlining, underemployment, food deserts, compromised healthcare access, the prison industry, genocidal wetworks, and on and on. In this, Black people have the horrifying underprivilege of being *mass mediatization's* most consistent public face of a comfort-control equation involving law enforcement and murder; and as such, we—along with everyone else—see Black people murdered and assaulted by police and parapolice vigilantes again and again across the country's news cycle with a sure-shot frequency.

That White Supremacy put me in a position to make this a reasonable conversation to have with my then–six-year-olds is a violence I will never forgive. I will go to work carrying it. I will share social space carrying it. I will form friendships carrying it. Yet I will not forgive it.

But back to the invitation. I've grappled with your request. Because, you see, I wonder: at what point does another piece triggered in response to the changing same become a part of the control-comfort ecosystem? This is complex in that writing such things is not cathartic for me and, I'd imagine, many others. Many different kinds of people could read what I've written, including people who are on the short end of the control-comfort stick. I wonder, and I wonder this honestly, when is writing about violence against Black people not a prediction, by which I mean: this violence is always happening, so when I wrote the poem I mentioned above, was I reacting to Watts, refracted through the historical pattern of the changing same? Was I acting in anticipation or response to the same thing happening again? Or was I, like the pastoral poet, not set on waiting for the Event of Fall in order to write about the redness in the arbor, but simply looking out my window, in some October, and watching a cycle continue?

Understand, I am angry, Editor. Not with the invitation, precisely. I am angry that a policeman murdered George Floyd. I am angry that members of my community must risk their safety—from more violence and a pandemic—to demonstrate against this changing same. But for this letter, dear Editor, I am angry that despite all I've written, alongside contemporaries who have written even better, adding to a tradition we carry on because it is the cycle in which our ancestors fell, suddenly red, to the ground and those who could, wrote about it also better than I; that what seems to be the case is that maybe if WE try again, maybe if WE write it more clearly and passionately, but not TOO passionately, or perhaps more passionately, or with more nuance, or perhaps with unequivocal statements, or more musically, maybe with greater eloquence, no, no, plain speech—that *maybe* if WE do that, juuuuuuust right and do it new and do it now with speed and urgency for those moments they are paying attention, white people will finally realize that *they are responsible for changing themselves*. And—via their massive, more sacrosanct voting power; disproportionately large economic resources; gross overrepresentation in positions of power; and, most importantly, prime access to their own psyches—for speedily and urgently dismantling the systems that exist for them and their privilege. And yes, class is critical to this, but more fluid than perceived race. Police don't check your credit rating before they shoot, club, rough-ride, or strangle your life away because, you see, they already know what they think you're worth.

So, I don't know what to write about this other than a police officer named Derek Chauvin murdered George Floyd, and Chauvin apparently had never done anything so unbecoming of an officer as to be permanently relieved of duty prior. Who, because several other police officers were present as he murdered George Floyd over the course of about nine minutes, apparently didn't seem to be doing anything unbecoming of an officer on Monday, May 25th, either.

I will write that Black people are being asked to be patient again and show faith that maybe this time will be the one that really makes a difference, even as the same old narratives about property damage roll out from the owners of stolen land.

I will write that again, my children are terrified, because this is terrorism. I will write that the president's vile White Supremacism doesn't let the brakes off of White Supremacy at-large, for to suggest so would require the ridiculous fancy that the train was built with any thought that it should ever have to stop.

I will write that if Derek Chauvin, George Floyd's murderer, is acquitted, the jury has agreed that $20 is the price of Black life. I will write that police will murder other Black people: some will be named Breonna, and some will be named Tony. Some will be children. Some will be elders. They will fall across the spectrum of gender identities. Many will be poor and almost all will be poorer than their white counterparts. The police will do this on and off camera. They will do it on the street and in the victims' homes. In parks and parking lots. They will do it, Editor. And they will do it *for white people*. Whether white people claim to want it done or not.

I would like to invite more white people to do something material about *not wanting it*. I would like to invite more white people to critically engage their sabotaging of our efforts through thoughtless, opportunistic acts of catharsis and self-serving gaslighting. I would like to invite more white people to stop preferring that we keep producing new work when it's they who have work to do. Isn't that desire the very condition that sailed many Black people here?

—Douglas Kearney, St. Paul, Minnesota

WHAT DOES IT ALL MEAN

Tish Jones

May (verb) [1]expressing possibility.
May very well have been our time or turn or time to turn the tithes
       of our lives lost 'round so it cost more
May as well not be matter to them, matter of fact, since they react
       less to knees on our necks than signs on our lawns

May (noun) one's bloom or prime; I guess this was our
May. Our bud to blossom and full body, blood red and enraged, our
       moment to be the thorn adorned our beautiful crowns. No

May (noun) fifth month of the year, in the northern hemisphere,
       will ever not hit us in our hearts, emulate attack and strike
       back all at once. be that as it

May (verb) [2]expressing permission, you
May survive this moment, go on. Gon' cuz they don't want you to
       imagine past the unimaginable that's why they play our
       demise on repeat, they wan repeat the past and get you back
       to beggin' "master,
may, I," but

may   be: time's up on that.   Maybe.

THE TRAUMA VIRUS

Resmaa Menakem

I'm a therapist and healer by profession. Partly by design, partly by good fortune, I've gotten enough people's attention to also be a cultural influencer. Yet none of this provided me with automatic immunity to a widespread virus—one that is older than America, and that has infected hundreds of millions of people for more than three centuries.

This virus, which I often call the *trauma virus,* was in my father's gene expression and in my mother's womb as I developed inside her. It was in the systems and structures of the world I was born into. It still circulates in my body, though my physical, emotional, and energetic immune systems now largely protect me from its effects. Nevertheless, I'm still an African American man doing his best to stay sane, healthy, and alive while navigating his way through the wilds of America.

My immunity did not develop naturally. Over the years—through practice, focus, and many repetitions of supportive body-mind activities—I've steadily built my discernment, my endurance, my stamina, and my immunity to this trauma virus, day by day and invited rep by rep.

I am not alone. Through the practice of Somatic Abolitionism, other people—people of all skin tones—are learning to build their own immunity, individually and collectively, to this virus.

This essay is an invitation to you to join us.

In the late 1600s, a group of powerful Virginia men, working together in a laboratory, created a virus and released it into the world. This virus was designed to protect, maintain, and increase these men's already substantial power—and to divide and repress any challenge to it.

This virus proved enormously successful—as well as both highly communicable and powerfully resistant to treatment. It quickly spread throughout the American colonies and infected most of its population.

Today, more than three centuries later, it continues to thrive throughout the United States, as well as in much of the rest of the world. It is literally in the cells of our bodies, the expression of our genes, the wombs of mothers, and the sperm of fathers. It is embedded in many of our institutions, our laws, our language, and our codes of behavior. It is ingrained in our habits, our norms, our assumptions, and our expectations. Over the past three and a half centuries, it has killed millions of people and injured or traumatized hundreds of millions more.

The seventeenth-century lab that engineered this virus was the Virginia Assembly. The virus it created and unleashed goes by many names—including the *trauma virus*—but the most accurate one is *white-body supremacy,* or *WBS.* Someone infected with the WBS virus can suffer from a wide range of symptoms. However, its two most prominent ones are:

* A sense that the white body is the supreme standard against which the humanity of all other bodies is measured and judged, both structurally and philosophically.
* A trauma response in one's own body to images, experiences, or ideas involving race.

The urge to otherize—to divide human beings into separate groups of *us* versus *them,* with *us* as worthy and spotless, and *them* as unworthy and dirty—is as old as our species. The Dead Sea Scrolls, which are close to two thousand years old, include a brief diatribe by an ancient sect in which it declares itself clean and holy, and its neighbors filthy and animalistic.

But what the Virginia Assembly did was a quantum leap in othering. It was a work of malevolent genius—and, arguably, history's most successful and enduring scam.

At the time, wealthy Virginian landowners faced a growing rebellion by workers—a rebellion that included people of many skin tones (and for whom those differing skin tones carried cursory advantages or signals). The Assembly created our modern concept of race, by legislating into existence two new classes of human beings: whites and nonwhites. The Assembly took away certain fundamental rights from nonwhites (Africans, the descendants of Africans, and Indigenous people from North America), while specifically granting those rights to all whites. The Assembly and its surrogates then spread this message to poor white Virginians: *no matter how poor or miserable you might be, you are better and more deserving than every nonwhite person on the planet.*

This strategy was spectacularly successful. Very quickly, working-class white laborers began to side—and identify—with their wealthy white oppressors and turned against their enslaved Black brethren. This quickly and efficiently dampened any rebellious impulses in poor whites—and helped to set in motion centuries of enslavement, violence, death, and trauma.

Today, this racialized trauma virus continues to express itself in our hearts, thoughts, words, actions, and decisions. We now also know that it embeds itself in many of our bodily structures; in the rhythms, flows, and vibrations of our bodies; and in our very cells. It becomes so much a part of most of us that it seems entirely natural and innate. This feature of the virus makes it hard to recognize. In fact, to many of the people it infects, the WBS virus is invisible.

The word *virus* is no mere metaphor. It spreads readily from person to person, and in 2015, researchers discovered that the WBS virus can be passed down from parents to children through the genetic expression of their cells.[1]

When someone experiences a trauma-inducing event, they may pass on their trauma to their children in multiple ways—women through the biochemicals in their wombs, men through the genetic expression in their sperm, and both through the ways in which they raise their kids. As a result, their children may suffer a variety of physical and mental health issues—without anyone understanding why. Evidence suggests that this transfer can continue for multiple generations.

The spread of the trauma virus is also literal rather than metaphorical. Like a coronavirus or a computer virus, once WBS finds a new host, it replicates itself over and over, then attempts to infect as many other human bodies as possible.

The WBS virus doesn't just infect white bodies. In the United States, for centuries, it has thrived in the tissues and thoughts of the great majority of bodies of all colors.

---

1. Epigenetics is the study of inheritable changes in gene expression. A landmark study demonstrating such changes in multiple generations of mice was published in 2014 by Kerry Ressler and Brian Dias ("Parental Olfactory Experience Influences Behavior and Neural Structure in Subsequent Generations," *Neuroscience* 12: 89–96). A year later, Rachel Yehuda published the first study to clearly show that stress can cause inheritable gene defects in humans ("Holocaust Exposure Induced Intergenerational Effects in FKBP5 Methylation," *Biological Psychiatry* 80: 372–80). For a more interesting and accessible read, I recommend Olga Khazan's article from *Atlantic Monthly* ("Inherited Trauma Shapes Your Health," at https://www.theatlantic.com/health/archive/2018/10/trauma-inherited-generations/573055/). Some background: in the Ressler and Dias experiment, adult male mice were given occasional painful electric shocks. A few seconds before each shock, the mice were exposed to the scent of cherry blossoms. The mice quickly learned to associate the smell with the shock that would follow. After a time, whenever the smell of cherry blossoms was released into their environment, the mice immediately freaked out. These adult male mice were then bred with female mice, none of whom was exposed to either electric shocks or the smell of cherry blossoms. Their offspring, none of whom had received or witnessed an electric shock, were then sprayed with the aroma of cherry blossoms. They immediately freaked out, just as their fathers did.

There six primary strains[2] of the WBS virus:

- * the **vehement** strain, which infects only white bodies
- * the **devout** strain, which infects white bodies almost exclusively
- * the **complicit, collective** strain, which is most common in white bodies but can infect bodies of any skin tone
- * the **progressive** strain, which also primarily infects white bodies
- * the **bodies of culture** strain,[3] which infects most bodies who are defined as nonwhite
- * the **African American** strain, which infects most Black bodies who have been raised on American soil

All six strains can create an acute, conscious awareness of whiteness as the supreme standard against which all bodies are measured. All six strains hold trauma in the body. And all six partly block the human body's normal impulse to emotionally grow and mature.

The central internal message of the **vehement** WBS strain is: *white bodies are the only bodies that deserve to live and thrive. All other bodies are dangerous. They need to be deported, segregated, incarcerated, or destroyed.*

---

2. There are other, less common strains as well. Like all viruses, WBS has steadily mutated over time and will surely continue to do so.

3. I use the term *bodies of culture* instead of *people of color* for three reasons. First, human beings are, as primatologist Franz de Waal notes, "bodies born of other bodies . . . . Bodies matter, which is why anything related to them arouses emotions." Second, the term *people of color* continues to otherize nonwhite bodies by holding them up against the implied norm of *white people*. In contrast, the term *bodies of culture* deliberately steers clear of any mention of color. Third, many people immediately resonate with the term in positive ways. Someone will likely complain that the term *bodies of culture* implies that white bodies have no culture. Of course every human being has culture, just as every human being has a skin tone. But no one imagines that the widely used term *people of color* (or, for that matter, *colored people*) implies that Caucasians have no color—i.e., that they are somehow transparent and look like the anatomical model the Visible Woman. Nor does anyone imagine that all *white people* have skin the color of chalk.

The core internal message of the **devout** WBS strain is: *white bodies are the best bodies. White bodies rule and deserve to rule. Being a grown-up means supporting and defending these principles by any means necessary.*

The defining internal message of the **complicit, collective** WBS strain is: *I accept white bodies as the norm and the default mode of humanity. I'll learn to work with this arrangement, and sometimes around it, as best I can—and I will do little or nothing to change it. In practice, this often means keeping quiet when I witness—or am harmed by—brief or subtle examples of WBS.*

The core internal message of the **progressive** WBS strain is: *no body is better than another body. But having a white body grants me advantages, and I accept these advantages without working to extend them to everyone. Being a grown-up means properly performing expressions of concern and agreement with bodies of culture, while protecting my own white advantage.* Currently, this strain of the WBS virus is the primary force that supports, maintains, and spreads white-body supremacy in America.[4]

The **bodies of culture** strain makes the sufferer constantly scan for clues about when, where, and how the standard of whiteness is (or is not) present; when and whether to challenge that standard; when and whether to lean into it; and when and whether to ignore it. This applies not only to events, situations, interactions, and relationships, but to the person's own assumptions, ideas, and bodily sensations. Perhaps most notably, it also applies to the conflicting desires to assimilate or stand apart; to seek borrowed advantages from white bodies or refuse to engage in such borrowing; to outperform white bodies or refuse to compete with them; and to define

---

4. I don't have the space here to explain how and why this is so. However, my frequent co-presenter Robin DiAngelo analyzes this in great and incisive detail in her book *Nice Racism: How Progressive White People Perpetuate Racial Harm* (Boston: Beacon, 2021). I offer a less extensive explanation in my book *Our Grandchildren's Souls: Protecting Ourselves and Our Descendants from the Racialized Trauma Virus* (Las Vegas: Central Recovery Press, 2017).

oneself in relation to white bodies or reject the act of defining one-self against others.

Someone with the **African American** strain (which most African Americans have *in addition to* the bodies of culture strain) is also constantly on the alert for danger, especially physical and emotional danger. This danger can come from any quarter: white bodies; institutions, laws, and norms; other Black bodies; and the sufferer's own WBS-driven experiences of doubt, inferiority, anger, and/or despair.

Underlying these six strains—and supporting and feeding them—is a low-level, persistent WBS infection that is present in America's air, water, discourse, norms, and, most of all, our bodies.

The primary symptom of this form of WBS is an acceptance of the supreme standard of whiteness—*and* the lack of a conscious awareness of that standard. This awareness is usually blurred, unconscious, or otherwise difficult for a person's cognitive brain to access. But it is present throughout their body, as a background stiffness or constriction. Although this form of WBS harms everyone, it provides specific advantages to white bodies.

Because this chronic infection is ubiquitous, we experience this background stiffness as normal. But of course, it is neither normal nor healthy. It is like polluted air or water that we take in constantly and take for granted. Meanwhile, it steadily harms our health and well-being.

Some white American bodies do not suffer from the vehement, devout, or progressive strain of WBS but do experience this background stiffness. These folks say things like, "I get along with everyone," or "I don't see race," or "I just want to raise my family and get along with my neighbors." They imagine (or pretend) that they are free of the WBS virus by attempting to sidestep the many conflicts and tensions it creates.

But the virus is still in their bodies. They carry it and spread it. And they continue to enjoy all the white-body advantages, while doing nothing to help turn those advantages into norms for everyone.

Until the WBS infection is recognized and treated—and until someone consciously chooses to adopt and repeat practices that enable them to heal and grow—they will pass on the trauma virus to others.

For many decades, most people looked at the disease of addiction as a weakness or a personal failing. They thought that someone became an alcoholic or an opioid addict because they were lazy, or selfish, or evil. We had similar ideas about people who suffered from depression, anorexia, obsessive-compulsive disorder, and a variety of other debilitating conditions.

Today we understand that these are illnesses that affect the human body, mind, and soul. We also understand that people who suffer from these diseases don't make conscious decisions to become addicted, or depressed, or anorexic, or compulsive. We have also learned to address these illnesses with treatment and healing, rather than with blame and derision.

At the same time, we firmly insist that anyone with one of these conditions act responsibly and accountably. Being an alcoholic is not an excuse to drink and drive. Having a compulsion to shop doesn't absolve you of the debt that your overspending accumulates. As an adult, you are still fully accountable for what you do, say, and decide. You are expected to learn from your mistakes, accept the consequences of your actions, and make appropriate adjustments, corrections, and amends. And you are expected to do what you can to heal and recover from the illness.

For many decades, we've approached WBS with the same kind of misguided ideas that we used to apply to addiction and depression. We point to someone infected with WBS, angrily accuse them of being racist, and expect them to change. This has proven as ineffective as walking up to someone slumped on a barstool, calling them a drunk, and saying, "Shame on you!"

We need to stop imagining that if we merely ridicule someone for showing symptoms of the trauma virus, they will spontaneously get well. Instead, we need to build accountability in ourselves and demand it from others. We need to learn and repeat practices that heal ourselves from the virus, encourage this healing in others, and help build our individual and collective immunity—while, at the same time, holding other adults fully accountable for what they do, say, and decide.

We study history to understand and learn from past events. Yet history always plays out in the present, in flesh-and-blood human bodies and minds. In the present, our mortal bodies experience fear, joy, love, shock, soothing, activation, and settling. As each new moment unfolds, vibrating with peril and possibility, each of us needs to act as wisely and compassionately as we can, never knowing what will happen next.

Throughout it all, each of us must grow up, over and over, step by step. We must hold our own—and each other's—feet to the fire. We must build our own discernment and resilience, and help others to do the same. We must repeat, again and again, practices that help us and others to heal and grow. We must drop the illusion that there are any shortcuts or workarounds—or that the responsibilities described in this paragraph apply to others but not to us. All of us—including asymptomatic carriers of the WBS virus—need to work to dismantle the systems, structures, norms, and habits that help it to thrive.

Let's get to work.

HOW WILL THEY TAKE US AWAY / HOW WILL WE STAND

Bao Phi

The protest is on Thirty-eighth and Chicago, at the site where a white cop murdered a black man, George Floyd. I am very familiar with this intersection: I grew up not far away, in Phillips, and currently live even closer. I'm not a regular, but I've stopped into Cup Foods for chicken, iced tea, the occasional UPS package held behind the counter. My favorite catfish joint is a couple of doors down. The Chinese takeout joint I sometimes order from, owned by a Black and Khmer couple, is across the street. The city council rep for this ward is a Black trans woman, Andrea Jenkins, who also happens to be an accomplished poet. I wear a mask and gloves and try to keep my distance, as my daughter had a fever this past weekend and we could not get her a Covid test until that afternoon. The protest is peaceful, and the organizers are trying to remind everyone to socially distance themselves responsibly. I can't concentrate. This intersection, central to my life and so many of my neighbors' lives, is the site of an unspeakably cruel murder of a Black man at the hands of Minneapolis police. Once again, people in the Black community suffer due to state-sanctioned violence.

One of the police officers, who stood and did nothing, was Asian. I wonder if Black people will look upon anyone from our race with anger; I wonder if Asian people will take the side of the police and anti-Blackness, or if we will see our own faces in his face and be overwhelmed with shame. I wonder if our communities will remember the coalitions among Hmong, Black, and other nonwhite peoples during the fight for Justice for Fong Lee, a Hmong teenager murdered by a white police officer who not only went unpunished but was awarded a medal of valor for it. I wonder if our communities will remember how Black people and other non-Asian communities showed up for us, and also, how Asians showed up at protests against the murder of Philando Castile, No DAPL (Dakota Access Pipeline), and other movements. I'm wondering if people will remember, as scholar Evyn Lê Espiritu Gandhi notes, that the American CIA recruited the Hmong, an indigenous minority, to fight against Communist forces in Vietnam and Laos. That the United States recruited Black, Latino, and American Indian men, often from poor neighborhoods, to fight against the same. I am not saying these movements or factors erase the complicity of this Asian cop. Nor am I trying to compare pain. I am saying this history exists, whether or not we fulfill its potential.

In the arena of social media, we take it out on each other. There can be a tendency to funnel very painful, intense issues through a personal lens. There are Black people who are saying some of the most racist experiences they've had have come from Asian and Arab people. There are Asians who claim that no one is pointing out how Black and other non-Asian people of color are enacting hate crimes against Asians during Covid. There are Black people who claim that Asians never showed up for them, so they would not show up for us. During the protests for George Floyd and Black Lives Matter, some Asians claim that Black people never show up for them, so they won't show up for Black people. And around and around we go.

It's all exhausting. Social media is, of course, performative. But I find it difficult to participate and witness the theater of it all when the day-to-day hits so close to home. Who is being genuine? Who is capitalizing on a profoundly painful, traumatic moment to make themselves look woke? Above all, who is actually being helpful? A

Black man is dead, murdered by a white racist police officer, in a system that carries with it four hundred years of anti-Blackness. What good is social media except driving one another crazy?

At first, I don't wake, because the helicopters and sirens are nothing new—not as a Vietnamese refugee survivor of war, which I am. And though they were perhaps not as frequent as they were in other economically impoverished and overly policed neighborhoods, choppers and sirens were certainly around in Phillips. So it's not until a bit later that I learn that parts of these neighborhoods are afire. The Cub Foods I worked at as a teen, pushing carts and breaking down cardboard for minimum wage, has been gutted. The urban strip mall, where I spent so much of my childhood waiting for my mother as she worked at the fabric store, is a burned and empty shell. There are rumors about who is responsible: local looters, because why not take things from these corporate giants' castles? Or is it organized alt-right provocateurs, capitalizing on this moment to push a race war? No, it's the libertarians, against big government. No, it's radical white anarchists, who want to burn everything down. One thing is clear: police officers are refusing to defend the community where those of us working-class and nonwhite people reside, will not protect the businesses owned by nonwhite people, families, immigrants. For my part, I don't fear the people in my neighborhood nearly as much as I fear armed white supremacists.

I'm worried about how my daughter will react. She was in the womb when her mother and I were part of the Justice for Fong Lee committee and the many actions we organized and participated in. She was seven when she marched with many other children for justice for Philando Castile. Now ten, she just picked out a teddy bear to leave at the memorial for George Floyd at the site of his murder, three blocks away from the community center where she went to preschool, afterschool, and the summer program before funding cuts ended the latter.

She is already afraid of police, that they may hurt someone she knows, or sometimes asks if they will take a family member and kick them out of the country. She once saw brown kids put in cages by

Trump's administration, turned to me, and asked if they were going to come and take her away. Months ago, a child had brought a BB gun to school, and the kids were forced to go into Code Red. Doors locked, lights out, hiding. My daughter, who has high anxiety, was traumatized. Now, whenever she hears a creak in the floor, water running in the pipes, or wind blowing against our window, she asks if someone is breaking in.

My father had written and illustrated an adorable page about his favorite childhood pets for my ten-year-old daughter. At the bottom he wrote, "This feeling of childhood only comes once, enjoy it!" I was going to go to our neighborhood Target to get a frame for it, but then almost on cue my daughter, who is doing an online check-in with her classmates, says, "Our Target has been burned to the ground," and I remember. She says this in a matter-of-fact tone, and not for the first time I wonder how many pragmatic survival mechanisms have been passed on to her. Her Covid test came back negative, and it's a sign of the times that this was not at the absolute top of my concerns.

Due to the unrest, the electric company cut the power in all of Phillips, which is where I was raised, and where my parents, both in the high-risk category for Covid-19, still live. During its heyday, Phillips contained the largest concentration of urban Indigenous people in North America. Every day was a reminder of the broken treaties and lies inflicted on the people who were on this land first. My dad, eighty years old, and a war veteran, uses a nebulizer to help with his asthma, but there's no power, and it's pollen season. He's been to the ER twice in the past five weeks. My sister and I talk and strategize. I offer to go to Target to look for a power bank that he can use overnight, then remember, again, the torrents of water running out of that Target into the parking lot from the sprinklers still running, fanning water from the ceiling to put out fires that have been extinguished for three days.

Years ago, I was struggling to find a place to live for myself and my daughter, in an unfriendly housing market where I was competing against dual-income couples. I was visiting my mom. She asked me how it was going, and what I was looking for. I didn't tell her I always think about all the places I had lived. Wherever the rent was cheapest, which meant my neighbors were always mostly nonwhite. The accidental fire I set when I was living in Section 8 housing, how my neighbors side-eyed me for making them stand out in the street while the fire department did their thing. I didn't tell her about the one place where a friend sent me hand-me-down bulletproof vests to stack against my thin walls, in the hopes they would slow random stray bullets. I mean, she still lives in Phillips. So I just said, I want to find a place where I can safely raise my daughter. My mom looked at me, scoffed, and said to me, in Vietnamese, "No place is safe."

As I type this, my neighbors and fellow citizens are protesting, again, in the streets. I am sitting tonight out, because my daughter is with me. My mother calls. I don't tell her about the times I have, and will, join the protesters. She doesn't like it when I protest in the streets, not because of anything political, but because as a Vietnamese person, she has seen firsthand that you can be punished for speaking out. Men in uniform, men with power, men with authority can take you away and your loved ones will never see you again.

Even though I don't tell her, she knows I go out there anyway. And she doesn't try to stop me. Both my parents have told me, throughout their lives, that it is important to stand for what's right. Both have told me stories about my ancestors, some of them troublemakers and dissenters, resisting French and Chinese colonial occupation. And then there's my father, who fought alongside the American soldiers, a fact many on the same side of the political spectrum as I disapprove of.

If all of this sounds contradictory, that's because it is. Sometimes I think being Vietnamese in America is to be an argument.

The next day we are informed that an armed militia of white supremacists was coming to our neighborhood to burn down the largely immigrant, largely nonwhite, largely family-owned businesses, and then do the same to our homes. There are emergency block meetings, neighborhood patrols, communication lines set up on Discord, which I believe is a platform where a lot of teenagers play video games together. I joke that most of Powderhorn is probably scrambling to Google to search "armed white supremacists are coming to my neighborhood, will my cats and chicken coops be safe?" Many of us are caught between wanting to flee the city to protect our kids and loved ones, or standing with our neighbors and friends and families against the terrible threat of these armed white men who wish to terrorize us. My daughter can't sleep, she sometimes cries, wondering if they will come for us. I can't sleep either, because I helped bring her into this world.

Days ago, another Black man was cruelly murdered at the hands of police. Here. His name, George Floyd. Again, George Floyd. The brutal anti-Blackness that is a cornerstone of this country continues, during a pandemic that disproportionately affects nonwhite people. And unfortunately, police brutality is not new to Minnesota. We remember Tycel Nelson. We remember that the killing of Officer Jerry Haaf at Pizza Shack, just a few miles from where George Floyd was killed, prompted the racial profiling and harassment of Black males between the ages of eighteen and forty in the early '90s. The brutal Gang Strike Force, which racially profiled thousands of American Indian, Black, Latino, and Asian men and abused numerous citizens. We remember Thurman Blevins, Jamar Clark, Philando Castile, Fong Lee, Map Kong, and unfortunately, too many more.

I asked myself long ago which side I wanted to be on. I keep asking.

I'll put my daughter to bed. As I do so, I know members of Black-led organizations will be up all night strategizing. I know my friends and fellow Asian Americans, in groups such as Rad Azns and Asians for Black Lives, will be organizing our people as well. I know Minnesotans of all races and ages will be putting out fires, sweeping up the streets, handing out food and water to one another.

Tomorrow will be another day I wake up and see the myriad communities I am a part of and care about doing their best to stand, support one another, and rebuild. To say, this man's life, George Floyd, this Black man's life, mattered. And this is where we live.

HEALERS ARE PROTECTORS / PROTECTORS ARE HEALERS

Marcie Rendon

I am an Anishinabe woman. I joke and say, "This is not our first pandemic, and it certainly isn't our first war." From smallpox to the Spanish flu to tuberculous and government medical experiments, the sterilization of Native women, and now the Covid-19 pandemic— Native people have survived it all. European folks arrived on the eastern shores with weapons we had never seen, and from day one we were target practice.

United States school curricula teach about the Cherokee's Longest Walk, but no mention is made of the other long walks Native people have been forced on—the Sandy Lake Tragedy in Minnesota or the Navajo's longest walk. After warfare broke out between white settlers and the Dakota in southern Minnesota, the Dakota were rounded up by U.S. military and interned at Fort Snelling on the banks of the Mississippi. They were living a bleak existence there when just a three short months after he issued the Emancipation Proclamation in 1862, President Abraham Lincoln ordered the hanging of thirty-eight Dakota in Mankato. During that same time Acts of Congress revoked treaties that had been made between the United States and the Santee Sioux. As a result, the Dakota people who had been interned at Fort Snelling were exiled, by state law, from

Minnesota. Forced to leave, they were taunted and spit on by white settlers who had been granted free occupation of Dakota lands.

In May 1863, thirteen hundred Dakota were put on steamboats and sent to the Crow Creek Reservation in South Dakota. In the first six months, more than two hundred tribal members died. This occurred a mere 158 years ago. No, certainly not our first pandemic nor our first war. The most recent time the U.S. government deployed arms against Native people was in 2016 at Standing Rock on the lands of the Lakota Nation in what is known as North Dakota.

Anishinabe people had a clan structure in place that, prior to European invasion, assured the protection, health, and well-being of our people. This system for our people is centuries old; it existed prior to our great migration. It is told in story that the Anishinabe people used to live on the eastern seaboard. An elder had a vision of food that grew on water, and he led people on a journey from the east to Madeline Island, where wild rice was found growing around Lake Superior.

The people brought the teachings of the seven clans with them. The seven clans are fish, marten, bear, deer, crane, loon, and bird. In recent times, the Eagle and Wolf clans are also recognized. Cranes and Loons are leaders, having different roles. Fish are thinkers and mediators. Marten are warriors. Birds are spiritual leaders and deer are peacemakers. Bear clan are both police (protectors) and healers. The clans are kept alive by a "living story," told in ceremony and community storytelling.

Imagine a world where the police (protectors) and healers are one.

The Dakota are known as the Oceti Sakowin, the Seven Council Fires people. They have a different system of assuring the protection, health, and well-being of their people. They have *tiyospaye* and *Thiwáhe*. This is a family system, with strict protocols, of knowing who you are related to. There is great shame, even today, if these protocols are knowingly broken.

These are the clan and family systems of just two tribes. Each tribe had, and many tribes still have, similar systems in place. Within these systems all children had a handful of people who cared for them. There were no schools. All children learned within the family and tribal structure. There were no orphanages. There was no mental health system. Living in harmony with your environment and with the people around you negated the stress that creates many of the mental health issues that have arisen in modern time. There were no jails or prisons. People grew knowing their own sovereignty. This means that people recognize that they are accountable to themselves for their own actions.

When people are nurtured in a collective community, when they are taught from birth their place and role and importance to the group—and they are taught to live with intact courage and integrity—there is little need for policing or the locking up of human bodies. If you look around the world, these truths hold for all tribal peoples I have heard or read about.

With the invasion of Europeans came Christianity and boarding schools. Our children were taken out of the home, out of the existing tribal clan structures and family. The clan system that protected children and where children were loved, cherished, and raised by a large extended clan family was decimated. Children were taken and raised by strangers who were not parents, who did not love or cherish them. These were people who were assigned to control, manage, discipline, and "take the heathen out" of the children. These were people who had taken vows of celibacy, vows to deny their human sexuality. As often occurs in such repressive environments, physical and sexual abuse was rampant.

In these institutions, Native children were exposed to horrific abuse. Although everyone was aware it was happening, it was done in secret. People were not allowed to talk about it; the adults did not admit it was happening. Children were separated from siblings. Children were not allowed to talk to others from their family or tribe. They were not allowed to speak their native language, so communication was cut off. Even if they wanted to talk about what happened to them, they most likely did not have the words for the experience of what happened to them—in their own language or in the imposed language. Children witnessed horrific abuse without any adult to explain what was happening, give them information, or process anything that was happening to them or the other children around them.

Many had also learned a new normal. Within the boarding schools and orphanges there was very limited healthy human contact. Physical contact was harsh, punitive, or sexual. In that kind of situation, any touch can be comforting in the face of the absence of caring, comforting, healthy, human touch. It can become the touch of choice.

Within Christian institutions and the belief systems around purity, virginity, and homophobia, children were indoctrinated into the shame-based identity of themselves that was attached to their sexuality. It also meant that there was training to be secretive about physical abuse, sexual encounters, and other aberrant behavior. Because the abuse happened in secret, with the awareness that it was happening—children knew that so-and-so was taken from the bed at night—children witnessed the physical abuse of their peers and were not allowed to talk about it. These patterns of keeping quiet about what you knew to be true and denial about what you were seeing became the norm for many. When situations like this occur continually and consistently, one develops an inability to tell what is or isn't appropriate; one cannot tell who is safe and who isn't.

There was more than one generation raised in boarding schools who never learned their clan and what their role was in the community. Within the clan system a clan member could not hunt or eat the animal of their clan. Because the Hudson Bay Trading Post of Canada wanted as many people as possible to trap furs for them, it was in Hudson Bay's best interest to destroy the clan system. It was systematically planned for the clan system knowledge to be disrupted through boarding schools and the introduction of alcohol, so that Indian trappers could be used to get furs without the clan restrictions. With this level of disruption, there were no safeguards within a clan system and a larger community that tracks itself. Also during this time, Native people were moved to reservations and were further isolated from their communities.

In one generation the clan systems were almost obliterated. These children, after years of abuse, were then sent home. They returned home where community mores and standards were no longer in place. The clan system and teachings, which previously had regulated all tribal life, were in tatters.

We know now that the children, and the adults who they were taken from, had to be suffering from complex trauma syndrome, PTSD, depression, touch deprivation, dissociation—in addition to untold other emotional and physical distresses. On return many of the children had lost tribal knowledge and the ability to speak their language. They did not know how to communicate with their relatives who they returned home to. Because they had been separated from their siblings—who in the clan system include biological and clan cousins—sometimes they returned home without the ability to recognize, actually recognize, the people to whom they were related. They probably did not have the language to explain what they had endured. Their trauma bond was with the other children who had experienced what they had experienced.

Following the boarding school system, and continuing on until today, is the forced removal of children into foster and adoptive homes. There is also the extremely high rate of incarceration of Native people. In Minnesota, the Native population is 0.1 percent. According to online records maintained by the Minnesota Department of Corrections, approximately 18 percent of the women in the state prison system are Native on any given day. For men it is 15 percent. We know that physical abuse, sexual abuse, and boundary crossing are common in correctional facilities.

The level of abuse, which was experienced by whole families, whole communities, whole swaths of Native people—in institutions from boarding schools to prisons, where it was normalized *and* made secret *and* made to be the "sin" of the victim—meant that people returned home without the words, or the knowledge, or the systems in place to help them recover from what had happened to them and those around them.

Children, raised in boarding schools and returned home, now found themselves in adult bodies that had been systematically rewired to heightened/hyper awareness of unsafe behaviors or rewired to the opposite end, to rigid aversion and denial of what people saw in front of themselves. With the clan and *tiyospaye* system in tatters, many of our people tried desperately to maintain the traditional ways, but it must also be remembered that we were forbidden by law to practice our ceremonies. So even if tribes previously had systems of healing in place, we weren't allowed to use them. The recourse for healing *and* the new enforcer were the same perpetrator—the Church.

After years of abuse, or enough abuse, one literally cannot see that it is occurring. The denial kicks in. People also have a hard time determining what is abuse. The uncle is a great-uncle. He spends all kinds of time with the children. That is what an uncle is supposed to do. The child is laughing and giggling in the bedroom. S/he is having fun. Nothing is going on. A parent uses a belt to whip a child. Skin isn't broken. It isn't abuse. Children are left alone to fend for themselves. No one is there to take care of them when they need help. It isn't neglect: *We came back in a few hours or a couple of days. Man up. Grow up. Don't show any fear.* All messages that were internalized in that boarding school era get passed down generationally and become the new normal.

Because so many people in our communities were abused and/ or have become abusers, many people do not recognize normal red flags. For many people who have been abused, body signals are confused with sexual arousal, with love, with care, with validation of their self-worth. Because so many people have been abused, their body signals of fight, flight, or freeze become confused and are read as "This is exciting" or "This is something to willingly engage in."

As a result, many people in general have no judgment to discern real danger. They have not had the safety, the protection, the right information for them to grow or to mature their ability to discern who is safe and who isn't, what is safe and what isn't.

One also becomes trauma-bonded to the abuser, or someone similar to the abuser. It feels like love, like comfort, like validation, like home, like normal. People with rewired senses become attracted, physically and emotionally, to perpetrators, offenders—people who do not have their best interests at heart. And people do not know how to leave these relationships, because we have been trained to take care of our own, not talk about what we see, not let others know what is happening. It is code passed down generationally.

Compound this with the forced removal of children for three or four generations. There is then an added fear, a real fear, that if one talks about any kind of abuse, someone will come in and remove either the children or the loved one, even if that person is the abuser. So whole tribes, whole peoples are afraid of talking, of speaking the truth—in fact are often encouraged to not talk about anything because *someone* will be removed.

And still we thrive. We become. We lead. We love. We nurture. The Native people alive today are the descendants of the 5 percent who were not killed off.

We have these learned behaviors that were never ours pre-contact. Many of us have worked hard to unlearn them. To learn new ways. Worked hard to undo these ways that are not ours, were never ours. We have strong language revitalization programs. There are children whose parents do not speak the language, who are becoming fluent in the language in immersion schools and are teaching their parents. Chemical dependency programs, both inpatient and outpatient, have healing modalities that focus on recovery from sexual abuse. These programs recognize the connection between chemical addiction and the need to numb the feelings and memory from past abuse. They recognize that to heal, one must recover from the trauma with an open heart and mind. Our treatment programs and women's healing centers focus on teaching and relearning the values inherent to our people.

Ceremonies, remembered and retaught, are held in Ojibwe communities in each of the seasons. There are more than ninety Sun Dances held in South Dakota when we are not in isolation due to the Covid-19 virus. Women hold full moon ceremonies each month. Sweat lodges exist in most communities these days. Connecting with ancestral spirit is necessary for healing and remembering to occur. Just as the historical trauma is passed down in our DNA, so is our resilience. Our bodies and spirits remember who we were before contact, before the trauma.

The seven clans of the Anishinabe are kept alive by a living story told in ceremony and community storytelling. More recently, these stories are being written down after having been passed down orally since time began: once again, the clans are fish, marten, bear, deer, crane, loon, and bird. In more recent times the Eagle and Wolf clans are also recognized. Cranes and Loons are leaders and have different roles. Fish are thinkers and mediators. Marten are warriors. Birds are spiritual and deer are peacemakers. Bear clan are both police (protectors) and healers.

There are deeper meanings to these sacred teachings of the clan system that are meant solely for Anishinabe people. In this time of Covid-19 quarantine and weeks of social unrest, Native people—in their bones and dreams—remember their clan teachings, even if they can't verbally name their clan: their spirits remember and they fulfill their roles with ancestral knowledge riding shotgun.

Imagine a world where the police (protectors) and healers are one.

THE PACHUCO HIMSELF CONSIDERS THE AUDACITY OF LANGUAGE

Michael Torres

There is nothing more to be said
regarding the wind's relationship
to the red oak trees. Except, perhaps,
that their branches haven't slept
in years, and those raindrops falling
leaf to leaf are not, in fact, a part
of the storm but what last night's
storm didn't get to say. I try not to

think about how quickly my daughter
is growing, how large a vocabulary
she has at six. Love could still be
a ball bounced back and forth
between us, could still be confettied
sunlight the leaves make across
our faces. This morning,

despite the quick clouds I watch
from my porch, I can tell you
which countries those gray formations

want to be; I can name the capital
of this moment. It never rains

when I visit my daughter. I return
to California, and I shouldn't be
surprised. But I am. And in the way
that I might deem funny after enough
years have floated by, perhaps when
I've accepted the town I'm living in
to be the one I will die in, and can
begin the slow process of forgiving it
for its failure to read sadness across
the faces of its residents. Our relationship,
my daughter's and mine,

sits sunny. On my shoulders, I tell her
to hold on; we make our way down
the block—as far as I've asked
to take her. She pulls at branches
and berries as we begin to speak.
Last time, she told me how small
her baby tooth looked in her hand
when it fell, how *peculiar*. I didn't
know how to tell her I had to leave

soon. I fear a season without trees to pull
conversation from, a time where there is
nothing left to describe, nothing left
to learn except how to say farewell
without seeming too eager, or worried
about upsetting the other. Don't say
we'll master that certain quiet, the kind
that accompanies leaving, and the moment
that follows that one, the one
I never have a word for.

COVID-19 AND ASIAN AMERICANS

David Mura

This essay was written two weeks before the mass murder in Atlanta on March 16, 2021, where six Asian American women and two whites were killed by a lone white gunman. The killer maintained he had no racial motive; instead, he claimed he was plagued by sex addiction and wanted to eliminate and take revenge on the sources of that addiction. But to the Asian American community, his attack was clearly based on both race and gender and was fueled by racist sexualized stereotypes of Asian women. These murders galvanized the nation's attention and traumatized the Asian American community. For many Asian Americans, a painful irony of this killing was that, for the first time in our lives, news about Asian Americans was dominating the media.

In certain ways, this is an essay I didn't want to write.

My reasons for not wanting to write about the rise of anti-Asian hate crimes, racism, and animus are, in one sense, beside the point: these hate crimes are vicious and unconscionable, and they have struck fear, anger, alarm, and outrage throughout the Asian American community.

The association of Asian Americans with the Covid-19 virus in the minds of so many Americans did not occur by chance. These attacks have been spurred on by Donald Trump and the ways he reveled in his rhetoric of the "Wuhan virus," "Wuhan is catching on," the "China virus," and the "Kung Flu," the latter eliciting rousing cheers and laughter at his rallies (other Republican officials used similar rhetoric). These attacks have been spurred on by Trump's positioning of China as a prime enemy to America (as opposed to his pal Putin and Russia), as stealing American secrets and jobs, as the real culprit in election tampering by a foreign power. These attacks have followed Trump's overall encouragement of racism, xenophobia, and anti-immigrant sentiment, by the ways he's dog-whistled his followers that they should freely express their white nationalism and shun any notion of "political correctness." And in doing all this, Trump has exposed a long-standing strain of racism against Americans of Asian descent.

Even as an Asian American, I'm taken aback by how quickly this anti-Asian animus has spread. In the past year (2020–21), there have been nearly four thousand reported incidents of anti-Asian hate crimes in all fifty states, a 150 percent increase. Activist Amanda Nguyen, founder of Rise, a sexual assault survivor advocacy organization, has compiled a viral Instagram video on the rise of anti-Asian violence. In one surveillance clip, an eighty-four-year-old Thai man, Vicha Ratanapakdee, is violently shoved to the concrete sidewalk by a masked assailant on a street in San Francisco. Ratanapakdee later died as a result of his injuries.[1] Nguyen told USA Today: "When I made that video I was tired of living in fear and I wanted to scream. It's so absurd that I have to say 'Stop killing us' . . . . We are literally fearing for our lives as we walk out of our door, and your silence, your silence rings in our heads."

When another elderly Asian man was beaten in Oakland, Asian American actors Daniel Dae Kim and Daniel Wu offered a $25,000

1. It turns out that Ratanapakdee's attacker was a young Black man; a few other incidents have involved Black perpetrators. The relationship between Asian Americans and African Americans tends to be highlighted only when there is tension between our communities; in the white mainstream press, focusing on that tension often serves as a way to downplay white racism. The anti-Black strain in the Asian American community and the anti-Asian strain in the Black community have complicated causes and histories, too complicated to go into in this essay, and I have written on this subject elsewhere.

reward for information that would lead to the arrest of his attacker. They wrote on Twitter: "The skyrocketing number of hate crimes against Asian Americans continues to grow, despite our repeated pleas for help. The crimes ignored and even excused." Manjusha Kulkarni, executive director of the Asian Pacific Policy and Planning Council, spoke of the trauma these victims feel: "So many of us have experienced it, sometimes for the first time in our lives. It makes it much harder to go to the grocery store, to take a walk, to be outside our homes."

In February 2021, on a New York subway, an assailant slashed the face of Noel Quintana, a sixty-one-year-old Filipino American, with a box cutter and left him bleeding. Quintana told ABS–CBN News that the attack seemed to come out of nowhere from the man next to him: "He started kicking my bag . . . . And when I said, What's wrong with you, and I moved away from him, that's when he slashed me." It's difficult to view photographs of Quintana with a huge scar running across his entire face and not instinctively flinch.

As many have pointed out, almost all Asian Americans know someone who has experienced anti-Asian remarks or violence in the past year, or they themselves have experienced it. I Google "anti-Asian hate crimes" and the "*New York Times*" and here's what comes up: "Attacks on Asian-Americans in New York Stoke Fear, Anxiety and Anger," "A Tense Lunar New Year for the Bay Area After Attacks on Asian-Americans," "He Came From Thailand to Care For Family. Then Came a Brutal Attack," "Why Has There Been a Spike of Anti-Asian Hate Crimes," "Spit On, Yelled At, Attacked: Chinese Americans Fear for their Safety." There's even a guide for teachers, "Lesson of the Day: A Rise in Attacks on Asian-Americans." In New York now, Asian Americans don't walk the streets with headphones, so they can be constantly on guard for a possible attack. Older Asian Americans are advised not to walk the streets alone—or even to go out in public. Asian American parents fear sending their children out of the house; some say they'll keep them inside even after the Covid-19 quarantine ends.

This rise in anti-Asian violence clearly needs to be better

reported and examined (the Trump administration downplayed such crimes and refused to investigate white nationalists and supremacists). Steps must be taken to prevent these crimes, from practical actions like community members accompanying elders to political organizing. There needs to be education about anti-Asian stereotypes and how anti-Asian animus always fails to distinguish between Asian Americans and various countries in Asia. Legislation is required to make charges of hate crimes against Asian Americans easier to prosecute. Placing stronger police presence in Asian American communities is being debated within the Asian American community. And all that's happening now needs to be viewed through the lens of white fears about their coming racial minority status and the rise of white nationalism. So much work needs to be done to dismantle the racist toolbox that has been in the arsenal of white supremacists throughout our nation's history.

And yet, it's only been lately that this rise in anti-Asian sentiment and hate crimes has begun to receive broad national attention. And that too is an issue. America has always been slow to recognize and acknowledge racism against Asian Americans, if it does so at all. And the rest of the time? We're invisible, we're the passing face in a crowd, in a commercial, or a television program or film. Blink once and you miss us—but of course you don't see us even if your eyes are open.

That's the painful irony underneath the pain of anti-Asian violence and hate: it's only when we're murdered or beaten or assaulted with racial epithets that the rest of America notices us. Otherwise we don't exist. And even when such crimes are committed against us, we still may not be noticed.

Last spring, as I was walking through the Mall of America, a reporter from the Minneapolis *Star Tribune* approached me. She was doing an article on the Covid-19 virus and wondered if she might talk to me. She then asked how my relatives in China were responding to the virus. I explained to her that I was not Chinese but "Japanese American." She next asked, "Well, how do your relatives in Japan feel about the coronavirus?" I explained that my grandparents came to this country around 1905, that we've lived here for more than a century, and we don't have any connections to relatives in Japan; all the relatives I know are here in America, are American citizens.

None of this made her perceive that I was offended by her presumptions. She didn't seem aware of her ignorance of the difference between Asian Americans or aware of our history or how she was assuming things about my background that ignored who I actually am. She was telling me what America has always been telling me: you're not really an American, you're not an American like a white person whose citizenship can never be questioned, who does not have to answer questions about where you are from or what those in Germany or Italy or Norway think. This reporter wasn't a Trump follower or a white nationalist, but she spoke to me armed with some of their same assumptions.

On a more general level, what irks me here is the idea that Asian Americans are only important if we're in the news. And we're only in the news if we do something awful—or when something bad happens to us. With the latter, that something bad is almost always connected with Asia. For one clear rule to being Asian American is this: if America has tension or bad blood or a war with a country in Asia, what happens next is a rise in hatred, fear, and distrust of Asian Americans. And it makes no difference if that particular country represents a different heritage or ethnicity from your own. Instantly, once this conflict occurs, all Asian Americans are lumped together, we all look alike (there is some distinction between East Asians and South Asians, who tend to be struck with anti-Muslim and anti-Arab bigotry). Just as importantly, our being part of America is contingent; we are never permanent Americans. We are instead permanently foreign, and that tune can surface whenever the sounds from Asia become discordant to American ears.

And yet, however minor, there's this discomfort I feel in writing all this. For within the general call for Asian Americans to speak out, I also feel in me something other than a pure and righteous political motive. What part of me wants to dive into the more obvious wrongs, the very real wrongs and crimes against Asian Americans, and ride that wave of relevance into what? My own relevance? I'm aware that my life, my daily concerns or those of other Asian Americans are most often simply irrelevant to other Americans. Why not grab this chance at the spotlight?

But how can I be irked by this when I myself write so often about the Japanese American internment, which is a prime example of how when shit happens with Asians, that shit gets dumped on Asian Americans? The internment is also a subject that can serve as a ticket to greater relevance; it possesses a historical significance that my own life does not possess and probably will never possess.

The question then arises: how do you connect the harms done to your community to your own individual life? I've led a relatively easy middle-class life, I've never been attacked or beaten as an adult for being Asian American, and the times I've been publicly insulted are few. True, I've experienced those subtle slights, slights you wonder if they're there or not, like when you're ignored by the counter person or someone is served before you or someone bumps you in a bar—and yes, there are deeper, more penetrating wounds I've experienced losing white friends or facing barriers in the literary world, but those are quite complicated and can't be reduced to a sound bite or a news story, and they don't possess the seeming relevance of anti-Asian hate and violence.

And what of the historical background of these anti-Asian attacks, a history most Americans, and even most Asian Americans, know little about? Tell me, reader, how many of these you're familiar with: the Chinese massacre of 1871 where a mob of five hundred whites and Latinx lynched seventeen Chinese; the 1875 Page Act barring Chinese women immigrants; the Chinese Exclusion Act of 1882; the nineteenth-century trope of the Yellow Peril; the 1924 Asian Exclusion Act forbidding all Asian immigration; the World War II internment of Japanese Americans; the fear of Communist Asians due to the Korean War; the anti-Asian animus caused by the Vietnam War, which then greeted refugees from that war; the 1980s' anti-Japanese auto industry animus and the killing of Vincent Chin, a Chinese American, by two white autoworkers (who served no jail time); the 1990s' anti-Chinese spy animus; the animus against South Asians from the first Gulf War to the present.

What's happening now is not new or unprecedented.

And all this brings me to a subject I *have* been wanting to write about—how do we approach America's racial history, how do we make that history real and connect it to the current moment?

For me, all this somehow relates to a project I'm involved in. These past few months, for Twin Cities Public Television, I've been working on a World War II documentary about Nisei soldiers (second-generation Japanese Americans). These Nisei solders studied the Japanese language at Fort Snelling, Minnesota, as part of the Military Intelligence Service (MIS). They ended up working as linguists throughout the Pacific theater, translating captured Japanese documents and messages, interrogating prisoners, guiding American forces on the battlefield. Their commanders estimated that the MIS Nisei linguists shortened the war in the Pacific by *two years* and saved a million American lives. Ironically, their cultural background, the very thing that made other Americans fear and hate them, became one of America's greatest assets in the war against Japan. In regard to their work, General Douglas MacArthur remarked that no army in history went to battle knowing more about their enemy. (In *The Art of War*, Sun Tzu extolls the value of such knowledge: "It is said that if you know your enemies and know yourself, you will not be imperiled in a hundred battles.")

This documentary is very close to me. My Uncle Tadashi was an MIS Nisei; so was Mr. Hoshizaki who lived on our block; so was Ike Yoshino, the brother of another uncle. And so, over and over, I've been listening to interviews with these MIS Nisei soldiers, interviews made when they were in their seventies or eighties. Some were from Hawaii, some from the mainland; with the latter, they and their families, like my own father and mother, were interned in concentration camps throughout desolate areas of the West, Southwest, and Arkansas. Many were kibei, that is, educated in Japan, some for a year or two, some for longer, and thus they were often more culturally Japanese than their fellow Nisei who had never lived in Japan.

These men were from my parents' generation, the children of immigrants, and what I find hard to capture in words here on this page is the tenor and timbre of the ways they talk about their experiences. The soldiers from Hawaii are a bit flashier, more outspoken, though not all; they come from a place where as Asians they're in the majority. But for the most part, all these Nisei soldiers display a sense of humility and a certain guardedness, a quietness that reveals . . . but only if you're perceptive, only if you can detect the nuances beneath their looks and words and tone. For there are depths they don't readily reveal even when talking about exploits of great danger on the battlefield or experiencing various aspects of racial prejudice: the knowledge that no Nisei could become an officer while less linguistically skilled white soldiers were made officers; the ways American troops would eye them with suspicion when they arrived in the Pacific; the knowledge that they might be killed by both Japanese soldiers *and* American soldiers; the fact that for many, their parents and brothers and sisters were imprisoned in internment camps behind barbed wire fences and rifle towers with guards. These men were—they've mostly passed—deeply patriotic, but not in any chest-pounding way, not in a trumpeting nationalism; theirs was not a patriotism that they might wear as a badge of great distinction and fanfare or a challenge to others, and certainly not as a testament to their masculinity. In some cases, it's almost a mumbled avowal: "I wanted to show that I'm, uh, you know, just as American as any, anybody. And this was one way to prove it," says Bill Doi, who eventually settled in Minnesota.

One of the more well-known MIS Nisei, Roy Matsumoto, fought with the famed Merrill's Marauders, the guerilla fighters who worked behind Japanese lines in the deep jungles of Burma. In the interview Matsumoto is in his late seventies, with wispy white hair receding to a high forehead, glasses. In a raspy voice, he relates a series of battlefield feats of great courage but in a manner that is quiet and matter of fact: when his unit is surrounded and running short of supplies and can't seem to find a way to escape, Matsumoto crawls through the jungle to hear the Japanese commander plan an attack from a certain direction; he then crawls back and directs his unit's machine guns toward the point of attack. The first Japanese attack is mowed down, but the second wave stops. So Matsumoto crawls back again to the enemy lines and tricks the Japanese, and his account is laced with a surprisingly dramatic energy as he spouts the Japanese phrases he used to imitate an officer in the Imperial Army as he ordered the enemy's troops to charge into the ambush. And his unit is able to survive and escape. But then his animated tone falls away into his normal, almost parsimonious and muted conversational voice, and there's no sense of bravado, no notice of his courage or even his cunning, but a sense of "I wasn't so special, I just did what any of us would do, what any of us soldiers were doing." And his smaller stature too, even compared to the other Nisei, belies the hugeness of his battlefield accomplishments.

In the interviews, I'll see something flicker across the face of one of these men, a feeling, an unspoken thought, and it's there and not there. Their emotions, their inner life are not, as they sometimes say in acting, highly indicated, and I have to strain to see it and sometimes wonder if I'm seeing it or making it up. The drama in their faces is not meant for the stage; it's not visible to the balcony or even to the front row. And perhaps it can't even quite be captured on film. At the same time, when one of them says the camps ended up breaking the isolation of the Japanese American community, I recognize an echo from my father about the camps, who had said something similar, along with how the camps weren't so bad (other Nisei held quite different opinions). And yet in his interview, this same Nisei soldier talks about becoming an activist in the sixties, protesting the Vietnam War, and how he looks back now at the internment camps and thinks, *Why didn't we protest more, why didn't we see how wrong they were?*—but he says this more as an aside rather than pushing the observation out and up front through either the tone or volume of his voice. It's not rhetorical the way he's saying it, it's not blatantly political: it's internal, regretful, rueful, slipped through in passing.

I don't know exactly where I'm going with all this. But it has something to do with the ways racial prejudice and hate crimes and the anger and outrage they provoke aren't the whole story. That there are ways the headlines, however needed, can flatten our communities, can make us more faceless, less individual, can turn us into another version of "All Asians look alike." I'm also trying to say that it's sometimes too easy for a younger generation to impose their politics or voice upon a different generation as sometimes younger activists try to do and as I myself have sometimes misguidedly done to the Nisei ("Why didn't you protest? . . . how can you say the camps broke the isolation of the community as if they were a good thing? . . .).

If I were to be a victim of a hate crime, at my age, sixty-eight, the headline would speak of an elderly Asian man. And though all three terms are true of me, they are hardly who I am—and certainly the term *elderly* does not refer to any way I think or feel about myself. And I guess that is, in part, the point I'm trying to make here: we are far more than what those outside our communities who hate or attack us have done to us. We are far more than a statistic or some story or headline in the news. And no matter how many news stories are written about these incidents, necessary as they are, they aren't sufficient. None of these headlines or stories will help others to see us through the lens of a specific individual, with an individual story and character and personality, to see us as something more than the current issue in America's racialized politics. For that, a different lens is required, and it is and isn't political. No, that is a task that can, in many ways, only be performed on an individual level, particularly by individual Asian American artists who, when they do enter the political, enter not through an opinion piece, but through the realm of art and the specificities of feeling and person and story that should be their prime focus.

LITTLE BROWN BRIEFCASE

Suleiman Adan

It only takes a smell, a picture, a random memory to bring me back to my childhood. A childhood that was immersed in hardship. Now I don't want folks to think I had a sad or miserable childhood. My mom made sure that my two sisters and I were always content.

The earliest memory I have of knowing that we were poor was when I was in sixth grade. It was 2006, and our lights got cut off. Now this wasn't a new thing. Our lights would get cut off here and there, but this was the first time I saw my mom look very worried. Usually, what we would do is fill the entire home with candles and pull out our portable DVD player and binge movies together as a family. However, this time instead of filling the house with candles, we gathered all the extension cords we could find in the house and connected them together, creating a snake-like cord throughout the house. We then went outside to the next-door house that was not sold yet and still under construction and found the outlet outside the house. Instantly, the house came to life again. I rubbed my hands together, trying to warm them. The leaves were beginning to fall. Autumn in Minnesota, my favorite season. I took a deep breath and walked back into the house through the back door. This instance was the first time I knew I was poor. This isn't to say that I wasn't poor before, just that now I *knew* I was poor. A strange feeling indeed. Having such a realization in that manner.

My mom is the most hardworking woman I know. A Somali immigrant. My mother has worked as long as I can remember. Like many children who were raised in poverty, I knew the value of money. I was indoctrinated at a young age. I was also taught about the "system." Growing up, all I knew about the system was that it made my mom stress out at the beginning of every month. Papers that she would frequently collect and keep safe. We children weren't even allowed to touch them. In a small brown briefcase under her bed she kept the documents. It wasn't until I was much older that I understood that the entirety of our family's financial history and security was housed in that little brown briefcase.

Now as an adult, I too house all my financial records in a small briefcase under my bed. Did I do this deliberately, or did I spend so much time growing up seeing my mom's documents in that briefcase that I thought that financial security was only attained by the aid of a brown briefcase? I honestly don't know. I am still working to figure out what financial security means. Do I even qualify for this "American Dream"? I think about this sometimes. How I will escape the clutches of poverty. Now I don't mean I am poor. Like many children of immigrants, our goal in life was to go to college so we could have jobs that could provide for our families. You may have escaped poverty; however, poverty is still part of your life.

Something that I had not realized about living in poverty was the impact it has on one's mental health. I think about the state of my mom's mental health working seven days a week and raising three kids by herself. What her mind must have been going through as she had to calculate how she'd use her EBT so she could stretch it throughout the entire month. What were her dreams like? She'd often tell me that she was too overwhelmed by financial hardships to recount dreams. Imagine that: life without dreaming. Sleep acting only as a reboot to tackle the day ahead. Dreams are supposed to be one of the very few guaranteed experiences human have, but they are a luxury for her.

How do those like my mom do it? Those who came to this country with next to nothing and still have next to nothing. How do they find the will to continue on, knowing that it is a hole that is nearly impossible to escape from? How do they continue to be so selfless and want to give more than they receive? Something my mom would say was, "We have a home, food in the fridge, and love in our home. Should we not help others so they can have that, too?" Truly astonishing. This mantra that my mom held is what I now live my life by. How can I say no to help those who ask for help? "No one has ever gone poor by giving," my mom would say. An astonishing mindset given her personal life and financial circumstances.

If there is one thing I would tell children of immigrants, it is to have the mindset that my mom had. To give selflessly. To want for others what you'd want for yourself. Sometimes we are quick to forget where we came from, what those who raised us had to go through to ensure that we did not need to endure what they endured. I would hate it when my mom would always tell me to become a doctor. There was no other career path that she would accept other than a doctor. It wasn't until now that I realized that she knew she could not offer generational wealth to help me as I navigate through life. However, she could offer a mindset, a lifestyle, an idea that could result in my becoming the beginning of generational wealth for my family. Now I may not want to go back to school to study medicine; however, I can continue to strive to climb the ladder of the American Dream and lay the foundation for generational wealth. But with one caveat: that my children and my family will continue to live by the mantra that my mother taught us. To give selflessly, to help others, and to always be grateful for what you have.

WE ARE ALL SUMMONED

Diane Wilson

When George Floyd called for his momma as he lay dying, the air grew still as it does before a storm. Only this one had been gathering for generations, holding in a terrible wrath and rumbling thunder that was unleashed with fire, with the sounds of sirens pulling every mother from her home, from her slumber, from her safe place. The summons was written on cardboard, a message that was heard around the world, a billboard the size of a woman's hands. He called for his momma, reminding us that he was somebody's child. In his moment of dying, all mothers were summoned to carry a message on his behalf:

Not another child.

Throughout history, and across continents, mothers have stood up in response to human rights violations, especially those that target our children. We have marched, protested, defended, and killed to protect them. We have served as truthtellers, as the conscience of a nation, as protectors of seeds to feed our grandchildren's children. And we have been forced to watch as our children were stolen, beaten, sexually abused, assimilated, and murdered in boarding schools, concentration camps, detention centers, and through relentless poverty. George Floyd's death was the breaking point in a war on children of color, a war that extends far beyond police brutality.

As fires burned throughout the Twin Cities from the violent out-pouring of rage and grief that followed George Floyd's death, the fragile food network that supplies much of South Minneapolis fell apart, exposing the vulnerability of elders and children already impacted by the Covid-19 pandemic. When Cub Foods and Target on Lake Street were closed during the riots, many people suddenly had nowhere to buy groceries, especially if they were dependent on mass transportation for their shopping.

The pandemic had already thrown many families into a panic when schools closed, especially if they relied on free school meals to help feed their children. Food banks like Second Harvest and many small food shelves immediately stepped up to help fill the gap. When the grocery stores closed, communities responded with heartwarming generosity by filling church parking lots with donated goods. Powwow Grounds on Franklin Avenue turned its gallery into an impromptu food shelf, staffed by volunteers.

In an apartment building for Native elders not far from Lake Street, the closing of these two stores was a hard loss for residents who were already struggling. At a time in their lives when elders should be honored and cared for, they were living on food stamps that did not provide enough food for the month. Some elders could not afford fresh fruit or vegetables or milk. They rationed toilet paper, made scarce by panic buying and hoarding. Cub Foods and Target were the closest, and cheapest, grocery stores.

Today, the alarms are sounding for escalating hunger that threatens to reach Depression-era levels. Food shelves are calling for more donations as they see a steady increase in families needing their support. Yet no one is asking why we allow the hunger of children and elders to be an issue for food shelves to resolve. No one is calling for the dismantling of a food system that is built around international businesses whose priority is profit, not people. Less direct than a police baton, or bullets and tear gas, our food system is yet another attack on the bodies of people of color.

When dairy farmers suddenly found themselves with a glut of milk after restaurants and schools closed during the pandemic, the *Wall Street Journal* reported in July 2020 that forty-three million gallons were dumped into fields before the USDA stepped in to purchase products for donation. Meanwhile, a marketing firm, Dairy Management, paid for by dairy farmers, has helped develop milk-heavy menu items with McDonald's, Taco Bell, and Domino's Pizza, among other partners. Thanks to this promotion, "on average, each American last year ate an extra pound of cheese and butter combined."

As Arapaho elder Ernie Whiteman once said, "If you can control the food, you can control the people."

In the weeks that followed George Floyd's death, I was mesmerized by television images from cities around the world as they erupted in protests, demonstrations, riots, rebellions, uprisings—whatever you care to name this revolution. I paid special attention to Portland, the city where my daughter and her family live. She had turned this historic moment into a lesson for her children, teaching them to show up at demonstrations, to speak out, to participate in the change that was happening all around us. As her mother, I was both proud and terrified to see photographs of her children, my grandchildren, as they marched holding their small, handwritten signs.

A few miles away, in downtown Portland, the Department of Homeland Security sent in federal agents wearing riot gear and camouflage uniforms to protect federal buildings from a weeks-long demonstration. A war veteran was viciously clubbed for trying to engage agents in conversation about their purpose, the oath they had sworn to support, defend, and uphold the Constitution. A group of mothers linked arms in front of the protestors, defying the agents to cross their line. Even as Oregon's governor and Portland's mayor demanded that the federal forces leave, unidentified agents driving unmarked vans began kidnapping protesters from the streets and holding them for questioning. When the victims were released hours later, they spoke of feeling terrified and fearing for their lives.

Congressman John Lewis, renowned for his civil rights work,

has warned us to learn the lessons of history to avoid repeating past mistakes: "Sometimes, I'm afraid to go to sleep for fear that I will wake up and our democracy will be gone."

The events in Portland, and other cities around the country, reminded me of a novel by Lawrence Thornton, *Imagining Argentina*, based on true history, that shows how humanity's darkest moments can be transformed by an act of courage, of imagination, of resistance. Embedded in the story, however, is the reminder how easily power can be corrupted and turned against its own people.

In 1977, when a young man in Argentina left home to run an errand and never returned, his family was unable to learn where he was taken, why he was arrested, or what happened to him. The military police often drove Ford Falcons as they seized citizens for questioning, arriving without notice in midnight raids while people slept, or taking them from their work so that they simply never came home again. The agents targeted anyone who was suspected of speaking against the military regime that had seized power in a 1976 coup. Many of the people who were taken were never heard from again.

Between 1976 and 1983, the military waged a civil war against Argentina's citizens, in which an estimated thirty thousand people were kidnapped, tortured, killed, and buried in mass graves. This was Argentina's Dirty War, a genocidal campaign intended to repress dissent by terrorizing its citizens and by creating mass fear and confusion. The media, ordinarily a watchdog that protects freedom in a democracy, was now controlled by the military. People were afraid to speak out in fear of seemingly random kidnappings.

The young man's mother refused to accept his disappearance. On a warm afternoon in April 1977, she organized a small group of mothers who gathered in the Plaza de Mayo in Buenos Aires, to ask the authorities about the disappearance of their children. Some came from small towns and were terrified of the police. Some women couldn't read or write. Their requests were ignored or met with silence. The police demanded they clear the plaza, as the authorities had forbidden public gatherings of more than three people. Instead, the mothers separated into pairs, arms linked, and began walking around the square.

They met every Thursday afternoon at 3:30, wearing white headscarves and carrying signs that bore the names and photographs of their missing children. At first, the military ignored them, calling them Las Locas, the crazy women. As the numbers of mothers marching continued to grow, the military kidnapped three of the founders, whose bodies washed up on shore days later. The week following the abductions, the Mothers who came to the square were met by police with dogs and batons.

But the Mothers continued to march each week, demanding information and the return of their children. They could not grieve without a body, without knowing what happened to their loved ones. As they marched, they kept the memories of their family members alive; they held up their photographs for the world to see. Say their names, say their names. Without guns, without riots, without politics, they demanded that the State return their children.

As international media brought the Mothers' March to the attention of the world, the military regime could no longer deny the truth. After the military was ousted in 1983, the Mothers continued to march, insisting on justice, even after the concentration camps were searched and no survivors were found. When a National Commission on the Disappearance of Persons held trials of the top leaders, ignoring the 1,300 armed-force members who were involved, the Mothers insisted on trial and punishment for all of the guilty. As long as any child remained unaccounted for, they would continue in their role as the public's conscience.

Uranga Almeida, whose son never returned from his errand, said in a 2012 BBC interview: "They touched the most sacred thing a woman can lose, a son. I was forty-five years old when they took Alejandro. I'm almost eighty now and I don't know what happened to him. I've been waiting all this time."

When Almeida's son was taken, all mothers were summoned.

All around us, in fields and rivers and forests, mothers have been standing up for their children, sharing a primal life force that animates everything, from birds to trees. These mothers are raising the next generation, feeding and teaching their children to become healthy adults. Our ancestors knew to pay close attention to the lessons they offered, as they obeyed natural laws that maintain balance between species and ensure survival by building strong communities.

The fields that surround my home near the St. Croix River open to a tamarack bog that has survived hundreds of years, possibly longer. The bog dates back to a time before this land was farmed, when it was a meeting place for the Dakota and Anishinaabe. As a complex, richly diverse environment, the bog is home to pileated woodpeckers, pitcher plants, and countless animals, including the whitetail deer.

In the marshy area that surrounds the bog, there are nearly two dozen dead stumps of white paper birch trees that have succumbed to age, disease, a changing climate. The ghostly white trunks have become snags for woodpeckers, owls, and bats who nest in dead stumps, feed on the insects attracted by the rotting wood, and hide food in their cavities. Nature is a conservator, finding a practical use for everything.

Two tall birch trees near the house have resisted whatever it was that killed the trees in the bog. The older tree has a double trunk, while the second tree has a single, slender trunk; both are about forty feet tall. The thin, peeling strips of white birch bark have been used by many generations of Native people for making baskets and canoes. I was reluctant to harvest, given the precarious health of birch trees on our land and throughout Minnesota, where they have been disappearing at an alarming rate.

A few years ago, the younger tree showed a worrisome sign of ill health: thinning leaf cover in the upper branches. When I checked the trunk, I found a large patch of evenly spaced bore holes, like a peg board, a sure sign of sapsucker damage. The yellow-bellied sapsucker drills holes in birch trees to feed on the sap, sometimes killing the tree by girdling it. More than half of the trees damaged by sapsuckers will die or succumb to the bronze birch borer that attacks weakened trees. By the time I checked my ailing birch, the damage had already been done. I could only wait to see if the tree would survive.

Over the next few months, the wounded birch remained stable, neither dying nor thriving. Instead, I saw a steady decline in the neighboring birch, the older, more mature tree, whose leaf cover also thinned in the upper branches. The secondary trunk withered and died. I was afraid that I was about to lose both trees. Through their dormant winter season, I waited anxiously to see what would happen in the spring.

To my great surprise, both trees leafed out with an abundant, gloriously green canopy. The younger tree bore scars from the sapsucker damage but showed no further sign of attack. Could it be, as I have often read, that the older, Mother tree shared her resources through the mycelial network that connects the roots of plants? A fungus made up of slender threads, or mycelium, creates a web that allows plants to share nutrients like carbon, nitrogen, and phosphorus. In a forest, Mother trees are often the biggest, oldest trees, with the most fungal connections, who often help their neighbors. That would explain the temporary decline of the older tree and subsequent thriving of both in the following spring.

This phenomenon receives both support and skepticism from the scientific community, who are reluctant to regard trees and plants as sentient beings. In the Dakota way, we consider ourselves as related to all living beings, Mitakuye Owasin. Trees are among our best and wisest teachers by modeling behavior in accordance with natural laws. While some scientists believe that the law of natural selection means that each tree is competing for resources against all the other trees—much like people who hoard toilet paper in a pandemic—trees actually thrive best when they evolve together, creating a healthy, stable forest. Just as in traditional Dakota communities, where kinship law is tribal law. As Ella Cara Deloria writes in *Speaking of Indians,* "The ultimate aim of Dakota life, stripped of accessories, was quite simple: One must obey kinship rules; one must be a good relative."

These relationships included water as our sacred first medicine;

the bison whose sacrifice provided meat, clothing, utensils, and tipi coverings; and the wild plants that became food and medicine. A long relationship with a wild grass, teosintes, evolved into maize, or corn, a food that could be grown and stored for times of hunger. Hunters, gatherers, and gardeners began their season with prayers and celebrated harvest with ceremonies of gratitude. Each person contributed their gifts and abilities to help sustain the health and well-being of their tiospaye, their extended family. This was the foundation for an indigenous food system that was centered in spirit and respect, and that supported the entire community.

Over the past several years, the birch trees have continued to thrive. Each fall, the trees drop their winged seeds, or catkins, to be dispersed by the wind. These tiny, fragile seeds are encoded with an astonishing ability to remain dormant, or asleep, until the right conditions are met for growth to begin. The moment of awakening, or germination, comes with the arrival of spring rains and a warming sun. The seed then feeds on the nutritional "lunch" that was packed by the Mother tree for exactly that moment.

In the world of plants that surround us, their survival depends on their ability to create a community where they can safely nurture the next generation. Like us, they need room to grow and clean water. Some will develop relationships with other species, like bees, who will carry their pollen to other plants. Some will communicate through pheromones that send warnings about predators. The wind will urge corn to grow strong roots, while the broad leaves of the squash plant will provide shade to preserve precious water.

And because of these complex, interconnected, collaborative relationships, we have food, shelter, clothing, medicine. We have life for ourselves and our children and our grandchildren. We are a species dependent on the gifts of plants. In a healthy, loving relationship, a gift is met with gratitude, with prayers of thanks. The natural law of reciprocity dictates that we provide gifts in return: clean soil and water, restraint, respect.

When we forget this law, when we break this relationship with the Earth, the Mother who nurtures all of humankind, then the door is opened to every other form of oppression. Racism is rooted in the turning away from our primal relationship to nature, which results in disregard for other species, for each other, for ourselves. The slaughter and near extermination of bison by white hunters in the 1800s created a stepping stone to boarding schools that were intended to assimilate Native children, to missing and murdered indigenous women, to genetically modified corn.

When George Floyd called for his momma,
the Earth as our Mother was summoned as well.

Dakota scholar and activist Harley Eagle once said, "I have to fall in love with the earth again and figure out what that means." Ultimately, he explained, when you're involved in antiracism work, results have to match the intentions. For the Dakota Oceti Sakowin, the intention has always been to raise beloved children.

Changing our society is slow, hard work. As we continue to protest, grieve, defend, and insist on a better life for our children, one of the ways we do this work is to dream a world that reflects our values.

Many of us share a vision where children grow up eating healthy, indigenous foods once again. Sharing food is a universal, joyful language that brings people together regardless of their differences, creating a true revolution rooted in Earth-centered kindness. Already, there are pockets of hope, of inspiration, of a future in which our communities reclaim our indigenous foods, restore the health of the soil, and protect our sacred water. Native chefs, including Brian Yazzie and Sean Sherman, have delivered thousands of beautifully prepared meals to elders and families throughout the Twin Cities. Dream of Wild Health—a Native-led organization focused on reclaiming indigenous foods—purchased an additional twenty acres to grow more organic food for the urban Native community, while teaching youth how to garden, cook, and reconnect with the cultural importance of these foods. Cities across the country are reclaiming unused urban land and building gardens, an act of resistance that heals the soil, our bodies, and our spirits.

When the challenges we face seem insurmountable, remember that we have a responsibility to do this work for the generations yet to come. During the forced removal of the Dakota from Minnesota after the 1862 Dakota War, women hid seeds in their pockets and the hems of their skirts so there would be food wherever they were being sent. They protected these seeds against soldiers, against their own hunger and that of their families.

This is our time to protect these seeds, the soil, and the water. It is our work to restore the dignity and well-being of the plants and animals that feed us. It is our responsibility to care for the most vulnerable among us.

As history has shown, a mother's love is one of the most powerful forces in the world, capable of bringing about great change. But this movement cannot be led by the mothers alone. We are all summoned to come together to rebuild our relationship with the Earth, our food, and each other, which is centered in spirit, reciprocity, and love.

> "... *each generation must do its part to help build the Beloved Community, a nation and world society at peace with itself.*"

> —Congressman John Lewis, 1940–2020

A TANGENT TO A STORY ABOUT THE SMITH & WESSON .38, OR, ATTEMPTS TO BE FULLY ASSIMILATED INTO THE WHITE AMERICAN PROJECT HAVE FAILED MISERABLY, IN THE FORM OF A SELF-QUESTIONNAIRE

신선영 辛善英 Sun Yung Shin

Q: When were you born?

A: I don't know.

Q: What do you mean you don't know?

A: My paperwork says May 12, 19＿, but it also says that was likely made up by the agency.

Q: What agency?

A: The social welfare agency.

Q: Where?

A: In Seoul.

Q: Why Seoul?

A: That's where I was found.

Q: Found by whom?

A: My paperwork says a policeman found me on the steps of his police station in Seoul at the _____ Police Box at 9 p.m. on January 9, 19__.

Q: What paperwork?

A: The paperwork that Holt International gave me when I went there.

Q: Went where?

A: To the Holt office in Seoul.

Q: When?

A: 2007, I think.

Q: You don't remember?

A: No. I think it was my third time there.

Q: How many times have you been there?

A: Six, including the time I was there from birth to leaving the first time.

Q: Why did you leave?

A: I was a-dop-ted.

Q: Why were you a-dop-ted?

A: Because I was a-ban-doned and had no family to raise me.

Q: Why didn't someone in Korea a-dopt you?

A: They didn't really do that.

Q: Why not?

A: Because paternal bloodlines are important. And it's shameful. Etc.

Q: Oh.

A: . . .

Q: Who a-dopted you?

A: A white Catholic family in a suburb of Chicago, Illinois.

Q: There's a branch of Catholicism called *White Catholicism*?

A: No. The *family* is, and still *are* white people.

Q: Did you stay in an orphanage before that?

A: My paperwork says I was in a foster family and that they had a dog and I liked the dog.

Q: Did you keep in contact?

A: No, my adoptive parents weren't allowed to know who they were, or to contact them.

Q: Why?

A: Everyone thought a clean break would be best for the child.

Q: What child?

A: Me, I guess.

Q: So what happened then?

A: I don't remember.

Q: Nothing?

A: I don't think so. But, the year after I was born, at the National Theater in Seoul, military dictator and self-declared "President for life" Park Chung-hee's wife, Yuk Young-soo, died during an assassination attempt on his life. A girl, Jang Bong-hwa, who was in the student choir present at this event for his speech was killed by a stray bullet. The gun used by the would-be assassin Mun Se-gwang, a Japanese-born ethnic Korean and a North Korean sympathizer, was a .38 caliber Smith & Wesson from an Osaka police box. This weapon is American-made and happens to be the most numerous hand gun on the planet. It's referred to as a "thirty-eight special." There are many notable facts about this gun. One mentioned in a certain popular online encyclopedia stands out:

> The .38 Special was designed and entered production in 1898 as an improvement over the .38 Long Colt, which as a military service cartridge was found to have inadequate stopping power against the charges of Filipino Muslim warriors during the Philippine-American war.

Q: . . .

A: . . .

Q: Well, okay. What else happened?

A: I became part of this new family and got a new name and stopped speaking Korean and I learned English.

Q: Then what?

A: I was naturalized as a U.S. citizen when I was five years old. (Before that I was a resident legal alien.)

Q: Hmm. Do you want to say something more personal? Do you remember anything?

A: No.

Q: . . .

A: No, I don't know my "real" name.

Q: . . .

A: No, I haven't found any Korean relatives.

Q: . . .

A: Yes, I've done two commercial DNA tests and have left my contact information with the agency in Korea.

Q: Why do you keep saying Korea instead of South Korea?

A: . . .

Q: Do you feel fortunate, you know, lucky to be an American?

A: Did Frankenstein's monster feel lucky to be resurrected even though he was made from the corpses of several dead men?

Q: Sort of? Not really. And isn't that kind of an extreme comparison? Why are you so morbid and weird?

A: . . .

Q: I think this interview is coming to a close.

A: Good. See you later.

Q: Oh, I forgot, do you speak Korean?

A: Some. More in my dreams.

Q: Hmm. How does that feel?

A: It feels . . . like the afterlife.

Q: Does . . . it feel good?

A: . . . Yes.

Q: Okay, now I'm done with questions, for now.

A: Good. I'm tired of answering these questions.

Q: Me, too.

A: I know.

Q: I love you. Don't die yet.

A: I love you, too. Okay. I'll try.

TODAY IN MINNEAPOLIS

Samantha Sencer-Mura

November 8, 2020. I am a person who can't serve a dish I have cooked without first telling guests what is wrong with it (overcooked, too much salt, lacking in presentation), and I have an inclination to do so with this piece. I wrote the following letter to my family and friends at the peak of the uprising following the murder of George Floyd. So much has happened in the following months, and it is easy for me to read this letter and criticize my past self—to find naivete where at that point I found hope, to find misunderstanding where I thought I had clarity and conviction. I feel the urge to give the caveats of hindsight as a foreword, but really, there is just this—I have complicated feelings of love for Minneapolis, and as I watched the city burn I felt compelled to put that love on paper. This is that attempt.

May 29, 2020

Dear friends and family,

I am writing to you all—many of whom do not live in Minneapolis—to let you know that first and foremost, as of now, myself, my family, and my loved ones are safe. Thanks to many of you who have reached out in the past couple of days. I'm also writing to help give some context for what you may be seeing on the news. The narrative you are hearing about what is happening to our community and our city probably differs depending on the news source. I know some of you are plugged into the same independent news channels I'm now tuning into, but for those who aren't, I wanted to give my firsthand account to accompany the images of devastation you are seeing on TV. I have never before felt so much like I am living through a moment in history. The least I can do is try and record.

I'm waking up today blocks from the Third Precinct where much of the protesting over the murder of George Floyd at the hands of Minneapolis Police (who have been fired but not yet charged) has been focused over the past few days. There is ash in the air from the fires. I am logging into social media and trying to get a sense of what in my community is still standing. The youth nonprofit I run is about a mile away, and I am getting emails telling me to board our windows. I am hearing that we should think about evacuating our house, that the fires are too close.

My partner and I have gone to the protests the past three nights. Our family members have joined us. Last night even my dad came out. At the protests, I saw a more diverse group than I have maybe ever seen gathered in Minneapolis. What I saw was that the voices at the forefront were mainly Black and Native folks, but around them and lifting them up were people of all races, ages, religions. When I left around 8 p.m. last night, the crowd was pretty calm, the police had retreated and were not agitating.

I got home and tuned into various livestreams of the continued protest. Around 10 p.m., the Third Precinct (the precinct of the officers who killed George Floyd), one stark symbol for injustice, started to burn. The police had come back and tried to again control the crowd and their space through violent agitation, but after failing, the mayor ordered the police to move out. They had given up. As I watched the videos, in the background I saw not only the precinct, but the small businesses that surround it—nonprofits, restaurants, theaters—also go up in flames. At the forefront, I saw and heard protestors—the majority of whom were very clear about why this is happening and what we want. The majority of the protestors also expressed regret at the fires and destruction of businesses. But everyone was clear—the problem is not the destruction; the destruction is a natural consequence of the injustice communities have been facing.

As someone who has worked in education the past ten years, one thing that stood out to me at the protests was how many young people were present and leading the action. It made me think of a proverb I used to have taped above my desk when I worked at a middle school: "If the youth are not initiated into the village, they will burn it down to see its warmth." Last night, I saw young people trying to get warm.

As an educator, my heart has broken many times over the past ten years for all that I am not able to provide or control for my students as I work in a system that was built for their demise. All the times I felt like my hands were tied. Like I was only making small positive changes, finding tiny interventions, creating a little bit of light in the darkness. As I watched my city burn, I heard the words and I watched the faces of youth who said, That is not enough. We had failed them. I had failed them. It was not enough. They have made that clear.

In my opinion, this uprising is the result of many compounding factors: four years of a Trump presidency, no convictions for police shootings, months of being cooped up in our houses due to a global pandemic as we watch the economy blow up, four hundred years of slavery, an empire built on stolen land.

Today, I am getting ready to leave my house, and I'm prepared to be heartbroken by what I see. Looking at the destruction, I know it can seem senseless. Part of me wants the protestors to have a plan, clear demands, maybe a clear leader. But capitalism is senseless. Black Death at the hands of those who are supposed to keep us safe is senseless. Witnessing Indigenous communities whose land we looted build encampments while I sit in a home blocks away is senseless. Having a president's tweet published with a disclaimer of violence because he has said that he is coming to kill us is senseless.

Do I want the properties I own and manage to stay intact? Absolutely. But what I want more is the end to systematic racism and unbridled capitalism.

We have looked our city in the face over the past few days. Minneapolis is a deeply unequal city: let us now see it for what it is. We can no longer say, "It's a great place to live, but . . ." or "It's a great place to live, if . . . ." It's not a great place to live. The things that make it great are built on the backs of the same people who are out there burning it down.

White supremacy has its own unique flavor in different locations, but it is prevalent everywhere. And I say this as someone who has lived in some of the most progressive cities in our nation. If you feel called to support the actions that are happening here, I have heard local leaders in the Black community and in the police abolition movement instead call for everyone nationwide to connect with the organizations and individuals doing that work in the city you live in and to support them. Two of them locally that I look to and admire are Reclaim the Block and Black Visions Collective.

The national guard is here. Five hundred troops down the street. I'm hearing we will have an 8 p.m. curfew tonight; people are warning of martial law. Please hold Minneapolis in your hearts today. If you are a spiritual person, please pray for us to find justice, without which we cannot have peace.

—Sam

LET ME TELL YOU A STORY

Melissa Olson

All sorrows can be borne if you put them into a story.

—N. Scott Momaday (quoting Isak Dinesen)

Let me tell you a story.

That Tuesday, May 26, 2020, I woke up to the news that another Black man had been killed by Minneapolis police. I read the story on my phone, but I wasn't ready to watch the video that accompanied it yet. I had gotten up early to prep for an eight o'clock interview about a project I had helped start six months before for MIGIZI, a Minneapolis-based nonprofit whose mission is to nurture the educational, social, economic, and cultural development of American Indian youth. The project would enable MIGIZI Communications to digitize and preserve their legacy radio archive, a project that encompasses fifteen-plus years of first-in-time radio programming produced by MIGIZI's First Person Radio program. The archive was stored on bookshelves inside a small utility closet in the center of the building and consists of approximately twelve hundred tapes and other miscellaneous recordings stored in cardboard boxes.

We had been awarded a small grant from the Minnesota Humanities Center for the project so decided to begin by digitizing twenty-four of the twelve hundred reels in the archive. While digging through the boxes, we came across a reel that was labeled "Prof. Momaday 1-3-77." This recording was unique because much of the archive consists of news stories evidencing the movements for American Indian civil rights and treaty rights, stories about AIM and the Red Power activism of the 1970s, and a social history of Native journalism of the era.

Upon digitizing the reel, we learned that, as we had hoped, it was a recording of Kiowa author N. Scott Momaday giving a lecture at the University of Minnesota in January 1977. A university librarian was able to unearth a reference to the lecture in an old *TV Guide* magazine that gave listings for weekly radio specials. The listing showed that Professor Momaday's lecture, "In Delight: The Character of the American Indian Oral Tradition," had aired on *The Saturday Show*, a production of KUOM, the university's campus radio station.

During his lecture, Professor Momaday referenced how his ancestors had survived bouts of epidemic disease in the mid-nineteenth century. His words seemed appropriate and necessary since we were now struggling with the daily realities of a new pandemic, the coronavirus, when the reel was discovered. I pitched the idea of reairing the lecture to producers at Minnesota Public Radio, and they agreed.

By the day of the interview, I had listened to the lecture several times in an attempt to describe it to Cathy Wurzer, who would be interviewing me on MPR's *Morning Edition* show. I wanted so badly to find the right words to talk about MIGIZI and our project, and about Professor Momaday's lecture. I am an experienced interviewer, I am co–managing editor of the MinneCulture program at KFAI Fresh Air Community Radio in Minneapolis. But I have less experience being on the other end of the microphone, so I was nervous. I fumbled through the interview as best I could as I explained MIGIZI's history and our digitization project.

MIGIZI Communications was founded in 1977 by a group of Native journalists and university students with a goal of countering the misrepresentations and inaccuracies about Native people in the media. The group chose the name *MIGIZI*, which means bald eagle in the Ojibwe language, because the bird signifies communication as well as guardianship and high standards. Those elements are what the group wanted the organization to aspire to throughout its history—excellence of communication, guardianship of the public trust, and high standards for reporting and ethics. Its first weekly radio production, *The Native American Program,* set the stage for *First Person Radio,* a nationally distributed weekly public affairs program that took listeners to Indian Country once a week until February 2018, when longtime host Laura Waterman Wittstock decided to retire the show. Today, First Person Productions is a multimedia training effort for Native youth aimed at providing state-of-the-art storytelling skills, enhancing self-esteem, and improving academic performance. Other MIGIZI programming addresses youth needs in jobs, culture, leadership, and more.

After the interview with Cathy Wurzer, I watched the video of George Floyd being murdered, and like everyone else, I was rendered shaken and angry.

Two days later, on May 28, I woke up a few minutes earlier than usual. The night before, my partner John and I had watched the Third Precinct set afire on national TV, and just the day before I suddenly realized how close MIGIZI's building stood in proximity to the center of the protest, just a block and a half away from the Third Precinct. I stood in the mirror nervously brushing my hair and trying to figure out what to do. I had to remind myself that I am the sole support for my aging mother, so as much as I wanted to join the protests, I decided not to, uncertain of the probability of contracting Covid-19 and passing it on to her. Instead, I picked up my phone and frantically scrolled through my social media feed to see if I could find an update on MIGIZI's building. A post by Binesikwe Means, MIGIZI's lead media specialist, confirmed that the building was okay.

I called Binesikwe and she said that the protestors and others had stayed off the street where MIGIZI was located, out of respect for a sidewalk clinic staffed by medical professionals treating injuries that protestors had sustained during the standoff with Minneapolis police the night before. Scrolling through my social media, I also learned that members of the American Indian Movement had stood guard in front of the building to protect it from fire and vandalism. Nevertheless, I told John that I needed to see the building for myself.

We jumped into John's van and drove from our home in Northeast Minneapolis. As we got closer to the building, the chaos was palpable. The air was thick with smoke, and I remember that it smelled like oil paint. We parked five blocks away and walked to MIGIZI as fast as we could. When we got there we saw minor tagging on the building's south-facing wall but, thankfully, it was otherwise untouched by fire—a fact we marveled at as we walked past the smashed-in window of Gandhi Mahal, the restaurant next door.

People everywhere walked slowly in twos or threes to survey the damage, some snapping photos of the property damage. *Fuck-12* in a ragged handwriting was tagged everywhere, and Black and Brown youths zipped around on their bikes observing people wandering around in shock and disbelief. It felt like kind of root shock, because nothing in the neighborhood resembled the orderly commercial corridor it had been just the day before. Debris was strewn everywhere we looked, and what was left of burned-out buildings was covered in soot. The streets were wet—not from water from fire truck hoses—but from spray from the broken windows where sprinkler systems had been set off. We stood for a few minutes at the corner directly across from the police station and watched a man standing on the other corner yelling into a bullhorn pointed at the charred Third Precinct: "Am I a Man? *Am I* a Man?"

We walked back to the van and cut slowly through alleys and side streets to find a way through the crowd that was beginning to reassemble. Once inside the van, John leaned against the door, lowered his shoulders, and set his chin. Then he looked over at me and said, "The building is not going to survive the night. If you are going to get the tapes out, we need to do it now." Thankfully, it was only ten o'clock in the morning, so we knew we had time.

When we got home, I called Binesikwe and we made plans to move the archive. Next I called KFAI and was given permission to store the boxes in an empty studio where they could remain through the night. John and I returned to MIGIZI an hour later with boxes. Undeterred by detours and traffic barriers, we drove up the alley behind MIGIZI and parked at the back door. With the help of staff members and teens from the First Person Youth Production program, we were able to quickly pack up the tapes and stack the boxes into the van. Then we took off and made our way the twenty-some blocks to KFAI. One of the teens came with us and helped haul the boxes up to the third floor to the studio we were given to use for the night. The young man was unusually quiet. Later, I learned that his brother had been killed by police a year before.

By the time we finished moving the boxes to KFAI the adrenaline had started to wear off and we were all hungry. We bought lunch at the sub shop up the block from KFAI, then drove another block over to the Augsburg University campus. We found a picnic table and sat down to eat. While we were eating, John looked up and pointed to a bald eagle that was passing overhead, having flown from the direction of the river. I have never considered myself especially spiritual, but seeing the bald eagle at that moment, the bird for whom MIGIZI named itself, left the three of us feeling reassured that we had accomplished our work for that day.

Just as John predicted, MIGIZI's building caught fire that night as embers from fires on either side of the building blew onto the roof. The executive director, Kelly Drummer, and her husband, Sam, and their daughter stayed in the building as long as they could. They called 911, but fire trucks never came. Soon they were told to evacuate.

The next morning, I returned to the radio station to check on the boxes and to make sure the room wasn't too hot or too humid. The sun was shining on them directly from the window so I covered the windows with newspaper in order to avoid potential damage to the tapes. And I learned from station staff that volunteers were forming a neighborhood group to keep watch from the roof to guard the building through the coming night. At that point, I decided to move the archive a second time, this time to my house in Northeast Minneapolis.

We moved the boxes later that afternoon, and for the next five weeks those thirty-three boxes of MIGIZI's archive took up twenty square feet in our small house between the living room window and my desk. It gave everyone at MIGIZI peace of mind. The boxes had traveled with the organization each time it moved in its forty-year history. Some of those years, the boxes must have been stored in basement cellars; they were caked in dust and smelled of decay.

I thought of the stories held on those reels, and of the journalists whose many hundreds of hours are recorded there. And I thought of community members, many of whom I'd known as a younger person, whose voices are preserved there. So as the weeks rolled on, I started to think of the tapes like an auntie or an uncle who had come for a long visit. Minnesota's stay-at-home orders and continued curfews meant that I rarely ventured outside. Home had become a place of refuge from the pandemic, but the boxes were stacked between my desk and the window—a physical reminder of the violence that took George Floyd's life and the violence of the fires that had destroyed parts of the city.

A librarian from Augsburg University reached out immediately following the loss of MIGIZI's building and asked what he could do to help. Appreciative of his offer, we decided to move the archive to Augsburg's library. It took me several weeks, but eventually I was able to create a basic inventory. I reboxed all of the tapes and drove them over to Augsburg's campus library. The precautions in place for the pandemic meant there was an empty classroom where they could be stored.

The Momaday lecture had been set to air on Thursday, May 28. It was understandably pushed back and did eventually air in the first week of June. I've listened again and again, and each time I hear it a little differently. There is Momaday in his booming voice quoting his fellow writer Isak Dinesen, reminding us, "All sorrows can be borne if you put them into a story. I am fond of telling stories; let me tell you a story."

There's not a week that goes by that my mom doesn't ask me over the phone how the project is going. The tapes are stored safely at Augsburg and are occasionally checked in and out by the archivist on our project who recently posted: "Today's adventures in archiving. Came across a few years of very poor quality tape that would not play back without squeaking/distorting. Froze my snack salami to cool the heads down and lower the friction coefficient. Fifteen minutes later, it played back like a charm!"

HERE BEFORE

Sherrie Fernandez-Williams

Not long after my mother's death, my pain receptors that are typically hyperaware became so overcharged that my body could barely take me where I needed to go. The large muscles, joints, and bones were all screaming for deliverance. Since traditional medicine provided no solutions, I signed up for a Qigong class at a friend's recommendation.

I sat on a mat, waiting for the instructor to begin leading us through the moving meditation, and questioned whether my black body, carrying the weight of grief, would find healing in a space where the cis, white, male instructor will profit from cultural appropriation. Surely, I would only tighten further, and the inflammation levels would multiply as the body does when it senses that something is wrong. But I was desperate for a cure, so I breathed out the unproductive thoughts and asked spirit to show me if I had no business being there. I followed the movement as instructed, shaking off unwanted debris, remnants of previous catastrophes. I held the energy ball in my hands and lifted it over me. I imagined bright, hot rays entering the top of my skull and allowed them to travel down my spine to my feet and back up again. By the end of class, my nerves quieted, and I felt more love and less disorder, so I decided to return.

On the next night of class, a substitute teacher welcomed us, a woman who spoke in warm tones. She smiled naturally, and she seemed abundantly comfortable in her loose-fitting clothing.

Something about her caused me to believe that she could transfer the gift of well-being to others. Besides, she looked like a beloved college professor from back in the day, which was probably the source of my immediate trust.

Along with leading us through moving meditation, she asked if we were open to her assistance. We all agreed. One by one, without touching anyone, she moved her hands around each person, pushing the energy down and away. I was last. She performed the same procedure, sweeping away the stuff I did not need. She lingered longer at my lower back, where my grief had settled. My mind dually held the feelings of skepticism and belief all at once, just as it did during the years I sat in church in my youth and earlier adulthood, but I could not deny that my body felt lighter and looser. She walked to the front of me, and as we stood face to face, she swept over my head, and I could feel the heat from her hands. She stopped suddenly.

"You have a lot of beings around you," she said.

"What?"

Again, she said, "You have a lot of beings around you."

Strong emotion usually accompanies my tears, sadness, joy, confusion, frustration, embarrassment, or shame—especially shame, but those tears came with a sense of knowing.

"I know," I responded. My mother and aunties, of course. My sister and brother, too, maybe? My grandmother, most likely? Who else?

My wife accuses me of choosing to engage with my dead relatives over those who are a phone call away. She is right. I do maintain a distance from the living, perhaps out of habit. But I long for them at the same time. There are moments when it is good to see family on social media. My cousin Irene records herself at her keyboard singing songs of praise to Jesus. She looks just like my mother, but she also looks like her mother, Juanita, and our three other aunts, Alice, Helen, and Eleanor, five sisters who started leaving us too soon; the last was my mother. I type at her. *You remind me of your mother at that keyboard.* Her mother, my Aunt Juanita who taught her how to play, lives in her fingers. *It is a blessing to give glory to God,* she responds.

My cousin and I are similar but different in significant ways. She is saved and sanctified. I am queer and "spiritual"—I guess. Instead of saying more, I play her next posted video. Her light touch of the keyboard targets an open wound. Then she sings, *Give myself away*. She repeats this line several times. Each time, her voice steadies, and her notes are safely carried through her device and out of mine. *Give myself away*, she sings. I never heard the song before, but the desire to surrender is familiar on a night when I'm reminded of what I am missing. Those to whom I belong.

I left Brooklyn at age twenty-three, and Mother soon began to slowly drift away, pulled by dementia. Five years later, there were few remnants of the mother I knew before I left town, and over the next fourteen years, I could not feel her presence, not even when I went home to visit. She passed away when I was forty-four, and remarkably, I began to feel her presence again. She was back, showing up whenever she felt like it, lecturing me about my less healthy habits—not drinking enough water, not getting enough sleep. I felt her with me while driving to work, shopping for groceries, and staying up late to complete tasks I could not get to during the workday. And if I stayed up too late, she'd start fussing like she did when I was a kid. I sensed that she just wanted to make sure I was going to be fine. Her presence made me feel like a teenager, the age when the elusive young person slips out of their parents' control and stops hearing their words of caution. After her death, I was listening to everything she had to say. For two whole years after she died, she barely left my side. Eventually, her visits slowed as if she was settling into her new realm with those who arrived before her. I began to get curious about her people, her past, her lineage, my people. I started searching, and soon by happenstance, I met a young black genealogist whose specialty is African American genealogy, which began with her own quest to know her people. With her help, I was able to make connections I was unable to identify on my own. She led me to family I knew nothing about, my Afro-Cuban family of Tampa, Florida. And with this knowledge, I began to recognize traits and behaviors as pieces to a puzzle.

I have always had a penchant for living in retrospect and was surprised to learn that a child can be born twice in my maternal grandfather's cultural belief system. To me, it makes sense that a blameless child would be allowed to return. My mother's brother lived for less than twelve months, left this world before he could fully realize that he had been here. Twelve months later, he was born again, as Alfonso II. My uncle's face formed in the mold of his father's, with skin perhaps from Nigeria and Cameroon, and hair perhaps of the motherland, indigenous Cuba, and the Iberian Peninsula. My uncle grew that Alfonso II mustache as an adult, wore high-waisted pants, stiff white shirts, and Panama hats. Going further back, was Uncle Alfonso the return of Angel, his grandfather? Along with the rebirth of blameless children, the souls of grandparents might desire to carry on. If they were good and deserving of more time, they might be allowed to embody the flesh and bone of a descendant.

Alfonso I, son of Angel, father of Uncle Alfonso, would have been familiar with this kind of coming and going since his youth. He had to have been the one to convince my grandmother that a baby can die and return. His little brother Matthias was the second coming of his big brother, Matthias. Alfonso I went from running behind big brother Matthias to keeping a protective eye on little brother Matthias when his mother, Rosa, had washing to do.

Matthias of the Bible was a replacement of sorts, replacing Judas as the twelfth disciple and appreciated for his ability to slip out of prison utterly undetected by the guards. Little brother Matthias, my great uncle, was not a replacement. He was he that lived first and last. In other words, the same dude.

Alfonso I and Matthias were grandsons of once-enslaved Africans, sons of Angel, born in Cuba, and nephews of Francisco, who was married to Delia. I can imagine two young couples, Angel and Rosa, Francisco and Delia, black Floridians at the turn of the century, committed to the Afro-Cuban-in-America ways of being as a means of survival. Their identities invisible, they might have tried to distinguish themselves from those who were once enslaved in the American South and those who were enslaved elsewhere. A white Southerner might look at them without that overwhelming guilt that produced murderous rage, the need to stomp out and erase their culpability by erasing those they have wronged.

Did Angel and Francisco believe their Cuban identity could protect them as other Afro-Cubans believed? Did they keep their wives at home and forbid them to work to make the differences clear? The wives of African American men often had no choice but to work. For a moment in time, a blip in history, perhaps a ten-year period in Hillsborough County, the employment at the cigar factories provided enough income for the wives of Afro-Cuban men to stay home with their children.

Was Angel the kind of man who made demands? I think of his descendants, Uncle Fonza and his four brothers. If we are duplicates of the same people coming back again and again, it is hard to imagine that Angel would be the type to make demands on his wife. My uncles were/are not the type of men who make demands, not Uncle Charles, who was on the receiving end of his first wife's violent temper. According to my mother, she was a drill sergeant in the U.S. Army with a fist like a rock. Uncle Milton only spoke in jokes. Uncle Fonza never charged enough for the window treatments he sold, and Uncle Sam said that he loved my mother the most because she never picked on him the way the other sisters did. Uncle Walter jumped in front of a train after coming home from fighting in Korea. The through line between them, decent and kind.

I can't imagine Angel raising his voice and using his male physicality as a means of control in his household. There's little evidence of this trait in most of the Fernandez men I've known in my lifetime. What I can imagine is Angel pleading with Rosa and making his case regarding how it might look to community members or the Euro-Cuban bosses at the factory. Would they have been viewed as Cuban enough if their wives worked at the factories or cleaned the bosses' homes? He would have tried to convince her that it was too dangerous for a black woman. Black women were preyed upon by the white bosses, and there was little her husband could do to protect her if he wanted to remain employed at the factory. Likely, Rosa would have conceded to her husband's plea. What else could she do?

Were Angel and Francisco early-to-rise pieceworkers who started their day in time to finish one thousand cigars before making it home for supper? Clean Havana makers enjoyed the luxury of flexible work hours more than a century ago because Vicente Martinez-Ybor wanted his employees to be fulfilled. When the international union of cigar makers desired a more structured day where employees got paid by the hour instead of by the cigar, the Clean Havana makers of Ybor City rejected the plan. It would have meant losing their ability to create a day of their own making. Martinez-Ybor believed that content employees produced a better product, so he allowed for flexibility, and he built a city to meet their needs. Cobblestone was planted on the muddy ground to inhibit the roaming alligator who preferred wetland over dry. Martinez-Ybor erected small but well-made homes, and in this town of immigrants, social halls were built for this community to gather and dance.

Were they at work during a Jose Martí visit and moved to action by the *Apostle of the Revolution,* the Cuban poet turned leader in the liberation movement? Did they belong to the collective of Cubans by way of Europe, West Africa, and the Taino—the Indigenous and Cubans who were a blend of all these people to varying degrees? They must have sat around the table discussing what it meant for them that Martí, who was white, would walk arm in arm with his good friend Paulina Pedrosa. It was an act of resistance and mobilization. Paulina Pedrosa, an Afro-Cuban woman born free but whose parents were not, commanded men to stand up for a decolonized Cuba. They may have been living post-Reconstruction when Jim Crow had the South by its throat, but Cubans of all hues had a common oppressor, Spain. Only unified people can beat a colonizer, and unity somehow required the denial of race, at least publicly.

Were Angel and Francisco two of Paulina's men? Is it even possible that they could have been beneficiaries of what this town had for its residents? At twenty-nine and twenty-eight, did they take their wives onto the dance floor and two-step to guajira? At least for a time, Angel and Francisco worked together and lived next door to one another. They had what was needed to live—no alligators, soulful employment, community, their casitas built by the town's employer who took a little out of each employee's pay to cover the cost of the well-constructed, shotgun homes where wives could spend their days with their children. Rosa lived with her cigar-making husband. Her husband, perhaps a member of Sociedad La Union Marti-Maceo, a mutual aid society, where they might gather with Afro-Cubans of Tampa and live in relative peace with Cubans by way of the Iberian Peninsula.

I think I choose to keep a distance from my living relatives because I know I have the propensity to ask strange questions, like which one of us might be our great-grandmother Rosa, our maternal grandfather's mother, the one who gave birth to seven children, but only two of which lived to be adults. I thought it might be Irene because she has more faith than any of us. *Faith is the substance of things not seen.* However, Irene's face was formed in the image of our maternal grandmother's people who immigrated from Barbados, not our maternal grandfather's people.

Of course, I would be the one to wonder if I am the return great-grandmother Rosa—even though I look like my father and his folks from Virginia by way of that North Carolinian tobacco plantation and the slave-owning Moore family. Still, I wonder if I could carry the essence of Rosa in the unseen parts of me. Although Rosa would have been better off returning through my cousin Val, college basketball star, later a detective, then later the owner of Val's Bar and Grill, an all-around badass. Or Aunt Juanita, because of her ability to galvanize everyone, bring us in one space, her family, her fan base. Or Aunt Eleanor because of her vitality. She was quick to laugh, tossing her head back like Dorothy Dandridge. Like Dandridge, Eleanor was cute and spunky and died too young.

I cannot discount myself completely. I carried no babies in my womb. When it was time to become a parent, adoption was the preferred option. When it was time to remove my uterus because fibroid tumors took it over, I nearly celebrated. If Rosa had the opportunity to do this life again, I imagine she would choose to avoid the risk of losing more babies. I live in retrospect, rarely in the present moment. I find nothing odd about the comings and goings of people, those who breeze in for a night, and those who return to do life on Earth all over again when there is more to say. Isn't there always more to say?

If I am my great-grandmother Rosa, she would know that there are other ways to lose. She would also know that there are other ways to love. She would know what it is to love and marry a woman. She would find comfort and acceptance in this love, and she would be so very proud of the love she found. She would be free to roam and to work. Lord, would she work! She would live way past the age of thirty.

Sometimes, I am more afraid of the living than the dead. I imagine sharing these thoughts with a cousin or sister, and the conversation quickly ends. My generation did not carry on the old ways of communing, because we love Jesus so damn much, and we're afraid.

I, too, am afraid, but I am more curious than I am afraid. What did they know? Do the number of chances we get to return reflect the number of misfortunes? If that is the case, every last one of us has had countless misfortunes.

My mother was four years old when she lost her father. My sense is that when she lost her father, his history went with him, part of her own identity beyond her grasp. She said nothing about Tampa and how her grandfather was an artisan who came to this country as a boy on a merchant ship but returned to Cuba at some point in his life. Did she know this part of her history that I learned from the genealogist? Her memories seemed to travel only to Bergan Street. What happened before Brooklyn seemed to be of little concern to her. My mother never knew of her grandmother Rosa, but she might have heard stories about Hattie, her grandfather's second wife. No one knew about Rosa, though it is her blood that flows through all of us.

For a precious moment in time, Angel and his brother Francisco were neighbors and worked at the same factory. For a time, Rosa and her sister-in-law were raising children just steps from one another. They must have all gone dancing together on Friday nights and met with friends in town, and surely there were friends. Surely there was laughter, hearty, knee-slapping laughter, and most definitely danc-ing. There was dancing in Ybor City after Cuban slavery, and black Cubans arrived in Florida to work. For a moment in time, my Florid-ian ancestors lived in a Cuban neighborhood and made Cuban cigars out of Cuban tobacco. This way of life would not last, but for a mo-ment in time, before Angel stopped making Clean Havanas, before he left town with only his boys after losing her, he and Rosa must have danced in Ybor City.

Faith comforts in times of loss. Angel and Rosa lost five chil-dren before those children could reach an age of discernment. If their faith led them to believe that we all get to return, then how many of them returned? Alfonso I fathered eleven children with my grandmother, if you count his namesake twice, ten if you count him once. His namesake lived a year, died, and returned, still his name-sake. In tracking Angel, I find my great-grandmother Rosa and am sad meeting her because she did not live beyond her twenties. It is hard to name the loss and even harder to claim it, for how does one lose what one never had? It is still a sad thing, more premature death in the family tree when I search for something a lot more satisfying. Yet, in other ways, I am enlivened by the discovery of her. Something in me knows that along with her five children who died as children, along with the first coming of my uncle, Rosa, a first-generation free black woman in America, was worthy of more time.

TRUTH, RECONCILIATION, AND FOUR MORE MEDITATIONS ON HUMAN FREEDOM

Arleta Little

1. Becoming

What within us is working itself out?
   Dreams. Yearnings. Genetic predispositions.
      Perspectives and reactions learned in childhood, in various conditions.
We carry so much within.
   What are we manifesting? What do we intend?
      Could a disruption or an intervention work to our advantage?
         And how can the grind of work become the grace of play?

There was a moment when this universe burst forth into being from the fecund void
                     (as it was called by ancients and ancestors)
or from dark matter
   (as present-day scientists say).
Some interiority, previously unobserved, manifested in a new material form.
The world as we know it ripened into being.
   And categorical departures have been part of its progression:
      From darkness to light, from inert to living, from bud to bloom,
            and now we, in the truth of our lives,
                  playing ourselves out.

2. Truth

Many resources can inform our inquiry,
        but answers are the dialectical work of each individual soul.
We can listen to our intuition;
    open to the guidance of ancestors;
        read the works of spiritual teachers, sacred texts, and philosophers;
            recite the words of poets and tell the stories of everyday people.
We can research the latest science;
    interrogate our lived experiences;
        talk to friends, family, colleagues.
And from this,
    we make our meaning.
From this, we must forge our unique expressions
        in this creative enterprise called life.
From this, we enter into sacred partnership with the Spirit.

3. Sacred Practice

We belong to life.
    We practice love.
Rooting in life and love secures our foundations.

From here, we subvert perverse paradigms and politics—
    countering callousness with care;
        countering greed with generosity;
            countering consumerism with connectedness;
            countering all forms of lovelessness.

Maturity is an embodiment and an enactment of love in service to life.

This is the movement.
    This is how we recognize progress—both personal and political.
        This is the incendiary practice of the sacred.

4. Victory in the Fire

In that moment before all hell breaks loose,
                we can find our peace.
We are told that in battle we find out what we're made of,
                but that's not the whole story.
Before battle, in the consciousness of what is possible, there is cultivation:
Morning after morning of waking up to the life that no one else can live for us.
We are careening,
     without complete control over the changes and conditions
                of our circumstances.
But we can know for ourselves what is necessary for integrity,
        what state of being we will choose to embody
                (indeed, all other preparations are incomplete without this).

Most human conflict falls short of the love offering that it could be.

For our part, we are aware that there is an emergence afoot.
    This may be the end of the world as we know it,

                but in our choice to be reconciled with this abiding moment,
                we gather ourselves, rise,
                    and go out to greet our guest.

5. Reconciliation

I am here at my own risk.

I am here honoring the history of my hurt and anger
    recognizing that more than hurt and anger are possible.

I am here to bear witness to your becoming;
    to witness the work that I cannot do for you;
        to welcome you to witness the work that you cannot do for me,
            but we can meet each other.
This creative opportunity
    will be what we make it
        and will be only as limited as we are.

We can be present for possibilities
and we can be as wild as our imaginations.

Herein lies the ability to create the world anew.

6. Community

We have common interests.
We have common needs.
If the existing structures do not meet our interests or our needs—
how then shall we organize?

If we rest in the knowledge that we are the alternative,
if we resist the temptations of authoritarianism and centralization—
what then becomes possible in the imagination of we the people?

Jazz.

Cultivated and spontaneous,
self-serving,
self-regulating,
self-governing networks.
Experimentation.
Evolution.
A multiverse of activity
(actions small and large)
that contributes to the collective vitality.
The Collective Vitality.
Not organization for the perpetuity of organization
but organization as an expression, a becoming,
as a conscious exercise of our power
on our own behalf.

DIDION DREAMS

Said Shaiye

You know, when you fall asleep, Allah takes your soul from your body, because neither your soul nor your body is yours to own but rather given to you on loan. And you know, when you wake up, it's only because He was generous enough to breathe your soul back into your body. So in that way, every day is a blessing and every night a test.

I used to dream of writing like Joan Didion before I knew who Joan Didion was, and I used to dream of living in Cali because all my favorite rappers praised it. The gloom of Seattle was never meant for Africans, so that Cali sunshine called to me like a siren song.

I'm sure it came as a surprise when my parents found me stuffing my life into a '97 Mazda Protege with shoddy brakes, four bald tires, no insurance, and a suspended license. I was ready to drive fifteen hours to pursue a dream I wasn't entirely sure of: spoken word poetry.

"Where will you live?" my mom asked.

"I'll figure something out," I replied.

"But you don't have a job, you don't have money, you don't even have a bank account."

"I know, Mom, I know. I'll be okay."

"Here, take this," she said, as she stuffed $400 in my hands.

I didn't say anything as I took the money and avoided her worried eyes. I told my family that I had a dream to pursue, that this dream involved microphones and stages, sunshine and pages. In reality, I was running to avoid feeling the constant emotional pain associated with borderline personality disorder. I would learn in California that no matter where you go, there you are.

I can't imagine how scared my mom was as I walked out the door on that rainy night, lightning spiraling against the Seattle skyline, a sheepish grin on my face. I can only ask Allah to forgive me for the years of hardship I put them through, for all the sleepless nights they endured while I was doing God-knows-what, God-knows-where. At the same time, I know that my suffering led me to do the things I did. I wanted the pain to stop.

Sometimes I have dreams that wake me up feeling guilty and ashamed, and inside my dreams I see guilt and shame and so I guess it shouldn't shock me that I wake up feeling the same shame. Which makes me wonder if guilt and shame follow me into my dreams. Which I guess they do. What I'm trying to say is that whenever I think of California, I think of regret. I wanted to make it as a spoken word artist—telling people I was frustrated with how few open mics there were in Seattle. I knew I wanted to write, but I felt the only valid way of being a writer was on a stage, not on the page. Excuse my Somali genetics—I come from a spoken culture. And so I spoke my memorized pieces, from Seattle to San Jose, carrying crumpled drafts in my back pockets, wearing the same pair of jeans so long holes formed in them, feeling like a beat. And I used to wear my Nike SBs, hanging out with skaters and drug dealers, talking about real problems, smoking real weed, looking real out of place.

I was too drugged up to care.

I was in too much pain not to drug.

My life in the bay was really all in my head. I paid $300 a month to sleep on a roach-infested couch in a two-bedroom apartment with six other Somali men. Most of them were taxicab drivers. I drove a pedicab for a living, so I guess that line of work is in our DNA. The first piece of writing I ever had published was about my experiences driving that pedicab every weekend in Los Gatos, Palo Alto, and Mountain View, hauling drunk clubbers around like cargo. It was demeaning as hell, feeling like an animal as these drunkards cheered and hoo'd and haa'd while I pedaled to pay my bills. On the weekdays, I mostly hung out at cafés and drank coffee, or stole wine and drank that in the park. Addiction is a terrible thing because it makes the addict feel like they're in control of their decisions.

At some point, tired of being broke, I found myself at an interview for a T-Mobile sales job at the mall. They wanted me to stand in this 3 x 3 box in the center aisle and yell at anyone who walked past, trying to get them to stop long enough to buy a phone they didn't need.

I walked into the interview and they asked me about me, and I said, "Hey. I'm Said, moved here from Seattle. I'm into poetry."

Oh, really?

Yeah, really.

Can you read something for us?

I said sure and recited a piece from memory, cuz real rappers always keep a 16 tucked. They clapped, I think, and I was hired. I told myself it was because I was such an amazing poet, but really it was an entry-level sales job, and they would've hired any warm body that came through the door.

Feeling elated, I walked to the parking lot and popped the trunk of my Protege. I pulled out a half gallon of cheap vodka, the cheapest they had, and started taking long gulps. It was acrid and steaming, having sat in my trunk for days, warming and warming in that Cali sun. And I drank and drank and drank, feeling it burn my esophagus as a tear floated down my cheek. I wonder why I have so much acid reflux now, as I conveniently forget those years of self-punishment.

I drove back to San Jose to celebrate with my friend B. He was from Philly, used to play ball at K-State before the racism chased him away. A cornerback, he was tall and quick and a natural athlete because his dad used to play in the league. Not having much else to do, I'd hang out at B's place in the middle of the day while his girl worked at Kaiser Permanente. We'd smoke together, laugh together, talk about our old lives and failed dreams. Shades drawn, choking on that Cali green. Burn, baby. All that celebration didn't really mean anything, because I walked out of that job in less than a week.

One night, B pulled up in a BMW he'd just bought, windows blacker than midnight on Broadway and Myrtle. We hit the town, some stupid club, got stupid drunk. I wasn't the flossy type, never could do the put-on-flashy-clothes-and-pretend-to-be-someone-else -at-the-back-of-the-club,

> shades on,
>> sipping on,
>>> sum'n *real* skrong,
>>>> song and dance.

Nah, I was just an alcoholic. I didn't drink for fun. I drank to numb. I smoked to forget that I needed to drink at all. And I popped pills to make it all feel inconsequential.

We were at the club that night because B was hosting some rapper's event and I was there for moral support. B was a spoken word open-mic host, and I always performed at open mics, so that's how we met. He always came to the events with his side chick, who had a thing for spoken word open-mic hosts, and I only know that cuz B told me her last two boyfriends were in the same line of work as him, which is a weird thing to notice about someone, but even weirder for that someone to have such a specific type of person who interested them, but I guess they both knew their place in the game and were okay with it. If only I could say the same for myself.

The thing about being a professional drunk is you don't ever really get drunk. Your tolerance is too high and there is very little laughter involved. It's a full-time job. You have to hate yourself from a deep place to drink every single day, no matter how much blood you throw up. It's kind of like writing, but with life-threatening consequences. I mean, writing is hard, and sometimes I wonder if writing is my new drinking, because you must have to hate yourself to put up with all the crap that comes with the writing life. But then I remember that the only thing more painful than writing is not writing. And so this is me writing to run away from pain, still running, all these years later.

I had a neighbor in Cali who was dying of cancer. He was old-school, 'Niners fan, muscle cars littering his front yard. He called me cub and I'd come over with liquor or beer or anything I could get my hands on. We would just drink and forget the pain of living. He often told me to turn my life around, that it was too late for him, but I still had time. I couldn't see it.

The thing about neurotransmitters is that they run out. A few months of hard drinking drained my body of all its norepinephrine, serotonin, and dopamine. Once I ran through those, as well as my money, I hit rock bottom. I looked up to find my totaled car parked outside the apartment after a night of casual drunk-driving. I didn't have any way to pay rent or to get to work. I'd lost all my friends because of drunken arguments. My food stamps were gone and my stomach clutched itself in emptiness and everything seemed very hopeless. I felt like dying that day. Not like dying-dying, but like: I just want all this to go away.

In California, they have this thing called a 5150 psychiatric hold. If a practitioner deems you're a threat to yourself or others, they can legally hold you against your will for up to seventy-two hours. I felt like that was the perfect way out: a three-day break from reality and from myself. I called 911 and the operator answered in that same monotone voice all 911 operators speak with.

"911, what's your emergency?"

"Yeah, I feel like dying."

"Okay, sir, you're having thoughts of suicide?"

"Yeah, I guess you could say that."

"All right, sir, do you have a plan in place on how you'd commit this suicide?"

"I don't think I have a plan, but I mean, I feel like dying, isn't that enough?"

"No, it's not, sir. We can't send anyone out to you unless we know you have a plan for taking your life. Otherwise, it's not considered an emergency."

"Wow. Okay, yeah, I have a plan, if that's what you need to hear."

"All right, sir, what's your plan?"

"I'm gonna steal some of my roommates' valuables and sell them at the pawn shop and use it to buy one gun and one bullet."

"Okay, sir, the authorities are on their way, just stay on the line with me."

"Sure, why not."

I continued to make small talk with the operator for another few minutes. Finally, I saw at least ten squad cars roll up to my block. The cops got out wearing Terminator-style sunglasses, pistols drawn, crouch-walking toward my position. At the time it didn't occur to me that they could have easily killed me, if they thought I had a gun. I've never owned a gun in my life, nor have I wanted to, but these things often get distorted across radio transmissions. "Plan in place to purchase a gun" could have become "Black man with a gun." I realize now that I could have easily died that day, that they could've mistaken my cell phone for a gun. But I couldn't think about that at the time. I just wanted help. I just wanted to live, but to do that, I had to tell them I wanted to die. This American life is an injustice in motion.

They screamed for me to put my hands in the air. They told me to have a seat on the curb. They asked if I had any weapons. I said no. They cuffed me, threw me in the back of the cruiser, and they asked me what it was like to feel like dying. I told them just fine, I guess. What's it like to take black lives with impunity?

That's the first time I ever found myself held against my will in a psych ward, though it wouldn't be the last. I walked out of that place on my twenty-second birthday, six days after I was admitted. A black Town Car waited for me on the curb and started the long drive back to San Jose. I asked the driver to stop before we hit the freeway because I needed to smoke a real cigarette. They'd only allowed me the patch or Nicorette gum while I was inside. He obliged my request and I started packing my box of Natural American Spirits. I lit one up, feeling the hot smoke go down my air tube and caress my lungs in a familiar embrace. I looked out at the rolling hills off in the distance and I knew that my little adventure had come to an end. I had made it a year and a half in the bay. My poetry dream died that day. It was time to go back to Seattle, to those cloudy skies, to that endless rain, to all that Othering that made me start writing in the first place.

A TIME FOR HEALING

Carolyn Holbrook

Strange as it may seem, I believe we are in a time of healing, though this may not appear to be the case. At least not on the surface.

Our planet, our bodies, our political landscape, in fact, the very soul of our nation were all brought to the forefront in 2020. Covid-19 was declared a global pandemic in March and became the largest and deadliest since the Spanish flu epidemic in 1918. Large numbers of hospitalizations and deaths continue to grow around the world, and, surprisingly, the United States is leading with the largest numbers of those hospitalizations and deaths.

Shortly after Minnesota Governor Tim Walz issued a stay-at-home order in an effort to slow the spread of the deadly virus, another pandemic moved front and center on May 25, Memorial Day. The tragic killing of George Floyd was the latest example of the uniquely American form of racism in which large numbers of unarmed Black men and women are murdered by law enforcement officers with no consequence to the killers.

The murder of George Floyd was so blatant and shocking that it woke the world up to this phenomenon that African Americans have lived with for more than four hundred years, since the first slave ship landed on the shores of Jamestown, Virginia, in 1619.

It is well documented that with that Dutch slave ship came the first law enforcement officers in America—groups of armed white men called "paddy rollers" who were organized for the sole purpose of monitoring and enforcing discipline upon Black slaves.

George Floyd's murder caused people around the world to stand up and demand the end of the decimation of Black bodies despite the risk of being exposed to Covid-19. But the murders continue. In fact, some that occurred shortly before the death of George Floyd were brought to greater attention. Most notably, the murder of twenty-five-year-old Ahmaud Arbery who was stalked and gunned down by a white man and his son while he was out jogging near his home in Brunswick, Georgia, and the horrific murder of twenty-six-year-old Breonna Taylor, an EMT who was killed in her own home by police officers who had mistaken her home for the residence of a drug dealer. Later, just three months after George Floyd was killed, twenty-nine-year-old Jacob Blake was paralyzed from the waist down after having been shot seven times by police in front of his children while trying to get into his car after having broken up a fight.

And now we come back to Minneapolis where on Sunday, April 11, 2021, another young Black man, twenty-year-old Daunte Wright, was gunned down by a policewoman who claims that she mistook her firearm for her taser. It happened while I was at George Floyd Square, the new name of the corner where he was killed, to celebrate the opening of the Social Justice Billboard Project, billboards created by three BIPOC artists.

The paddy rollers are still alive and well. There is no doubt that many more unarmed Black men and women whose names we may never know are being shot and killed regularly. Meanwhile, Covid-19 rages on, an epidemic that was fueled by our past president who deliberately created the negative environment we are living in today. Even before he was elected in 2016, he continually encouraged his followers to undermine the peace and hopefulness that Barack Obama's presidency brought to the world. He started the "birther" movement in which he claimed that President Obama was not born in America and encouraged his supporters to believe that Obama was a Muslim, which, in his eyes and those who think like him, is code for terrorist. He also inflamed unrest by denying climate change, systemic racism, and the coronavirus, even going so far as to make the pandemic a political issue, undermining well-documented science and discouraging his supporters from taking care of themselves and their loved ones by doing the three very simple things that will help to get it under control, even mocking individuals for wearing masks and maintaining a safe distance from others, and blaming local governments instead of climate change for wildfires that have raged in the western part of our nation.

Still, I maintain my belief that we are in a time of healing. It became clear in the early days of stay-at-home orders from many governors when the air became cleaner, less polluted. Today I believe that, more than at any other time in history, we have an opportunity to finally heal our hearts and the inbred systems of racism and economics that cause food insecurity, health disparities, educational achievement gaps, housing inequities, and more—we have an opportunity to heal ourselves and the Earth.

Even though we are living in a time of crisis after crisis, I can't help noticing that nearly every day I get at least one email from someone who is offering healing in some form or another. There are healing meditation circles everywhere and a growing number of dialogue circles where participants are more willing to be real in their conversations about the difficult matters around social justice. More Than a Single Story is one of those organizations. We presented a virtual panel discussion with BIPOC healers who practice a variety of modalities. We were both surprised and not surprised that more than three hundred people were in the audience. And poets, writers, and visual artists, many who felt blocked during the early stages of the pandemic and after the George Floyd murder, are now creating beautiful works with words, music, and visual art.

The results of the 2020 presidential election have shown the world that the American public is yearning for a return to decency, democracy, racial justice, environmental justice, and truth, a reckoning which President Joe Biden and Vice President Kamala Harris are calling for. It will not come easily: there are still plenty of people who prefer discord and will continue to attempt to obstruct rather than promote justice and peace.

I believe strongly in the healing power of the arts, which is often quiet. People regularly ask what led me to become a writer. The answer is easy. I was the quiet one in my family. My journal always listened, even when the louder voices overpowered me. Now, as a writer and a teacher of creative writing, I use the quiet power of words to tend to this healing work. Also, as an arts activist, I enjoy bringing people from disparate racial, ethnic, and artistic backgrounds together, using the power of the arts to create environments of civic literacy in which BIPOC writers along with other artists and individuals from nonartistic disciplines can discuss issues of importance to them in their own words and their own voices.

Kindness, compassion, and respect prevail in these powerful conversations that are often quiet, and audience members from many communities engage with us. The public discussions are often followed by writing workshops that invite participants to explore these topics with other interested people.

I love the word *tending*. It implies kindness, compassion, and remaining steadfast in the face of injustice. It shows that we change the world through our everyday actions whether those actions are teaching, writing, or the daily passage of our life experience down to the next generation. That tending is often quiet. While others are making their voices heard, healing is taking place quietly and steadfastly. I recently saw an anonymous quotation that has been sticking with me: "Sometimes it's not about the act of praying, or what you think or say when you pray. Sometimes it's about what you learn while waiting for the answer."

SPEAKING INTO EXISTENCE

Kevin Yang

It's been nearly a decade since I first started writing and performing spoken word poetry. Looking back on my life, I am grateful for the places that my art has taken me. However, I am most grateful for the ways that my art has allowed me to look inside myself. I think about the multiple identities I inhabit: Hmong, American, man, second-generation immigrant, introvert, anxious, artist.

Through my art I've found the language to discover and love myself in times when loving myself seemed like an impossible act.

I am the son of two parents who escaped Laos and Thailand as refugees and who eventually found their way to Minnesota. I was born and raised in South Minneapolis during the '90s at a time when most Hmong families either lived in North Minneapolis or Saint Paul. Finding my place as a second-generation refugee Hmong kid in a predominantly white neighborhood and society was a challenge.

I remember being a very sensitive child who cried often. I excelled academically, but I was easily overcome by my emotions. From an early age, I was told to stop crying, to man up, to have a stronger heart. I was bullied regularly. I was physically beaten and made to feel ugly and stupid. At the time, I wondered if this was normal, something that brothers and boys just do to one another, but looking back on it as an adult, I recognize the abuse and trauma from such moments that left scars that continue to ache to this day.

I found it difficult to share myself emotionally with others and to trust people. Even though I found it difficult to open up, I never stopped taking things in. I continued being an extremely emotionally sensitive person, but I had no healthy ways of releasing these feelings. The feelings welled up inside of me, and they destroyed my self-confidence, unsure if the next person I'd meet was going to be someone I could trust or someone who was going to turn on me. It felt like my emotions, my anger, my worries, my sadness, anything other than happiness, were burdens that I had to carry, and to share that load with others was a selfish act. Do not let them see you cry, do not let them see you get angry.

I developed social anxiety. I found it difficult to make friends. I continued digging into myself. Our family moved around a lot when I was a teenager and that made it even more difficult for me to practice building social relationships. I didn't grow up with many close cousins and didn't meet other Hmong kids my age until the tail end of elementary school.

Although I was aware at a young age that I was different from my white peers, I didn't feel racism until I shared a classroom with other Hmong students for the first time. Gangs were a present force in the Hmong community when I was in elementary and middle school, and it was something I watched many of my Hmong friends fall into. For many, it was a way of finding belonging and a way to take care of each other. When I moved schools, they were the first to welcome me. I was an academically gifted student, and I was deeply conflicted, having to choose between this feeling of belonging or my academics.

My new friends would often get into trouble. They didn't pay as much attention in class. They goofed around. They were your typical sixth graders. My teacher knew how seriously I treated my academics and wasn't happy that I was being influenced by them. I remember my sixth-grade teacher giving me an ultimatum: I could continue sitting by my Hmong friends or I could choose to be more academic and sit on the other side of the classroom with the more well-behaved kids. I chose the latter. For the rest of the school year, I sat on the opposite end of the classroom, and I couldn't help but see the physical and metaphorical distance growing between myself and my Hmongness.

It was around this age that I started feeling a deep shame about being Hmong. I'd turn on the television and hear about Chai Vang, the Hmong man in Wisconsin who was convicted of killing six white hunters after being confronted at a deer stand on private property. I'd flip the channel and hear another entertainment reporter cracking jokes about William Hung on *American Idol*, remembering all the comparisons I had to deal with at school. I'd flip to the next channel and hear about a Hmong gang shooting that had just left three dead. It's a reminder of how powerful narratives can be. All I understood Hmong to be was what I saw on the television and what I heard in the classroom. It felt like to be a Hmong man was to be violent, to be ugly, to be foreign.

I committed myself to avoiding all things that I associated with being Hmong. I joined the football team. I participated in debate competitions. I took all the AP classes I could fit into my schedule. In nearly all of these situations, I was the only Hmong person in the room. There was a sense of pride that I felt from that, like I was transcending my Hmongness. Like I was beating the odds. There was an obvious association I was making between moving closer to my academic goals and moving further from my Hmong identity. Looking back on it now, it's easy for me to name it for what it was, internalized racism.

Despite finding academic success and value in my new activities, I continued having a difficult time building relationships with my mostly white peers. I continued dealing with social anxiety, feeling like my race was the reason why no one could understand me. I didn't trust my voice or opinions, and I continued being so full of feelings that I couldn't process.

For as long as I can remember, I've loved storytelling. Even before I knew what letters were, I'd doodle cartoons with speech bubbles popping out of their mouths having imaginary conversations that I'd interpret for myself. Writing stories was a way that I articulated all of the angst and trauma that had been living inside of me. I kept stacks and stacks of journals, but these were always stories that I kept to myself.

My junior year of high school was a turning point. I took my first creative writing class, and it was a decision that probably saved my life. Up to that point, I had seen writing as an intimate and personal act that I didn't share with anyone. It was the first time in my life that I was being asked to have my work critiqued by others. There is an art form to getting an entire classroom full of angsty teenagers vulnerable and courageous enough to share, and our teacher was a virtuoso.

For the first time in my life, I was in a space where I felt comfortable sharing all of these feelings that had been sitting inside of me. It was the first time I felt like my feelings weren't burdens. I received so much love from my classmates and my teacher. It felt like my feelings were important even if they were difficult. I remember vividly reading my responses to warm-ups and quick writes and hearing snaps and seeing nods in the room and feeling affirmation that I had been craving for so long.

The first thing I wrote for the class was a play about a son who meets his estranged father for the first time in decades and they get into a polite argument that escalates uncontrollably. All I could think about after writing it was where did all these feelings come from, where had they been lying? I wrote a short story about a zombie who misses his still-living lover. I wrote a poem about how I was self-conscious of my smile and how I wanted braces. I imagined worlds for myself and populated them with characters. I was proud of myself. Most important, I was so proud to be sharing these stories with others and hearing stories from others in ways that I had never been able to do before. What a magical act that is, to create a space where other people dealing with their baggage could share and feel for one another with words and worlds that they created. It was a reminder that my feelings were valid and that my art gave me language where language was difficult. I cannot thank my creative writing teacher enough, not just for teaching me how to become a better writer but for teaching me that I had a voice worth listening to.

The first time I read another Hmong voice in literature was in my twelfth-grade English class. We were in a unit covering *The Things They Carried* by Tim O'Brien, and my English teacher had the wherewithal to assign a reading that included voices that weren't just white. I remember reading a poem from the teacher's selection and feeling shook. I can't remember the name of the poem, but I remember how it made me feel, reading Hmong words and Hmong experiences that resonated with me in ways that no other piece of literature had ever done before. I immediately raised my hand and gushed on and on about how important the poem was to me. It was only about twelve lines long. The class moved quickly to the next subject, but after class my teacher sensed how important that moment was for me and insisted that I read a book of poems called *Real Karaoke People* by a Minnesota poet by the name of Ed Bok Lee.

I remember taking the poems home and devouring them, over and over again during Christmas break. The audacity of the language, the sharpness of the narratives, the voice I heard echoed in my head. It cut so deep and so close hearing the complexities of what it meant to be Korean American.

I joined the speech team during my senior year of high school. The way that my category worked was I had to find a published poem that was about seven minutes long and perform it. The poem I chose was "The Secret to Life in America" by Ed Bok Lee from the very book that I had just spent an entire two weeks consuming. I laid the poem out on white printer paper and glued it on to thick black construction paper and for weeks did everything I could to memorize the words, repeating the beginning lines over and over again:

My brother sits me down and tells me
the secret to life in America.
I'm twelve years old when this happens.
He grabs my shoulders and says:
No one likes an immigrant.
It reminds them of when they fell down
and no one was around to help them.

For three months, I did my best to embody the poem at every competition I performed at. In many of these competitions, I was the only person of color in the room, performing in front of mostly all-white audiences in tiny rural towns across the state of Minnesota, performing a poem about a young boy trying to make sense of the contradictions of being Asian and an immigrant in this country.

I remember searching for Ed Bok Lee on the Internet and finding a video of him performing the poem that I had spent three months carrying. There was a certain rhythm to his poem that I would learn was called slam poetry and spoken word. I continued searching online for these new ideas and finding videos of other Asian American poets creating work that blew me away, like Bao Phi, Beau Sia, and Kelly Tsai. Their work was fierce, sharp, and such an authentic reflection of their identities. I knew almost immediately this was what I wanted to do.

As an Asian American and a Hmong American, I find few opportunities to see myself reflected not just positively but authentically by mainstream media and literature. It was a reminder of how important it is for communities to tell their own stories on their terms. It left me hungry to create my work and further tell my stories using this medium new to me.

I wrote my first spoken word poem, "Cry for Us," as a dedication to my grandmother who at the time was very ill. I watched videos of my favorite poets on repeat, trying to capture their rhythm and ferocity. It was an emotional experience, creating something that I knew was designed to be heard out loud. I was scared, but I was excited. I performed it at a multicultural student group presentation in my high school's auditorium. It was the first time I had ever performed my work in front of an audience like this, outside of the safety of a classroom, outside of the ruse of a competition.

They called my name and I came out from the back of the stage to a microphone looking out at an audience of about one hundred other high schoolers. I could feel my voice trembling, but I continued every line of the poem that I had memorized. I remember the applause as I walked backstage and shook hands with the host and walked off to the bathroom. I remember crying myself to tears after the performance. The poem was a love letter to my grandmother and everything that she stands for. It was a poem about my love for my Hmong culture and the fear of watching a generation of knowledge disappear with her. It was the first time I had ever written about what it meant for me to be Hmong.

I graduated from high school and moved to Saint Paul to attend college. Although I had found opportunities to share and write with others in high school, moving to Saint Paul was the first time I had ever felt like I was a part of a community. I joined a collective of Asian spoken word artists called Speakers of the Sun and learned how art could be used to mobilize. I performed at protests and actions. I joined slam poetry teams where we honed our writing and performance together. I taught and led workshops where art provided a platform for other young people to share their struggles and celebrations. For an art form that I create alone, I am grateful for the community that surrounds me.

At many points in my life, when I was struggling with something, I'd ask myself, how can I turn this feeling into a poem? The past few years of my life have been a reminder that I can't art away all of my problems. I still struggle with anxiety and self-esteem and sharing my feelings, but I've been finding new ways to take care of myself. I started going to therapy for the first time, trying to process my traumas and eager to learn about how I can show up as a more authentic and healthy version of myself in my relationships. I'm in a loving relationship with a partner who reminds me to be the best version of myself, that I am worthy of love and capable of sharing the love back. I don't perform as much as I used to, but I know that this art still lives within me and I am grateful for all it's done for me. I am alive because of it.

THE WEIGHT

Ezekiel Joubert III

I'd been living in Los Angeles for eight months when a wave of homesickness began to come over me. The consistent warm weather, morning mountain views, and golden sunsets no longer cured my longing to be back in the wetlands of my small rural community in Sumpter, Michigan. The spring semester had just ended, and the isolation from the coronavirus pandemic lockdown and the mass uprising following the murder of George Floyd made me miss home even more. This year was turning out to be one hell of a year—the extraordinary, unexpected, and unforeseen would surely define our state of knowing, being, and doing. Home has always been a source of regeneration, but the weight of this work seemed impossible to carry.

I anticipated a call from my mother. We spoke twice the day before about the hospitalization of Mathes, her brother. My family had just visited him two days before to celebrate his sixty-third birthday at the assisted living facility where he had lived for the past two years. The stay-at-home order prevented them from going inside the building. So they presented him material and sentimental gifts through the glass. Although a ghost of his former self, he expressed thanks with his same ole smile as he threw up the peace sign.

"He's gone," my mother said. What do you say to someone who has experienced so many untimely familial deaths? I am not usually a person without words to express how I feel. But the uncanny feeling of *I know* somehow remained buried in my chest.

Deep down, my soul had been preparing for a family passing. Something about knowing what brings death close makes you feel it when it's near. Though I prayed that we would all survive, I knew this was inconceivable. Although most folks decided to cancel their summer vacations or flights home out of fear of the virus, I decided with many of my fellow passengers that mourning cannot be done alone.

"Flights these days force a brother to learn how to pack light." That's always my response to my family when they ask me, *Where's the rest of your luggage?* Back when I first left home, a question like this would have received a defensive response. I was young, black, gay, and running away as far as I could. I had learned in college two lessons. One, in order to be successful, out, and free I would have to move to a bigger, whiter, and gayer city; and two, I did not have to put up with anyplace that didn't accept me. It would take years to recover from these dangerous life lessons. The fractures they made, filled with assumptions, forced me to paint my family with broad strokes. On the flipside, I have lived away from home for more than fifteen years now, and most of those years I struggled financially. Taking cheap flights that only included a personal item—room for a couple of outfits, a computer, and some books—saved me lots of time and money.

Today, it is more of a ritual.

This trip, though, felt different. We are living in the midst of one social crisis after the next. For months the majority of us have been witnessing all of it from our couches, on streamed cable television or social media, doing our best to convince ourselves that the state of lockdown could never be a permanent reality. Wasn't it Orwell who warned us about Big Brother? A warning we have ignored for the sake of technological innovation. I guess it's too late to go back to the good ole days without our tracking devices stuffed in our pockets. The lockdown and physical body searches (that never cease to happen when I fly) are weapons in the arsenal of state power.

These days it seems like the state is all-powerful. The public displays of police dominance, blatant disposability of poor and working people, and disdain for the unwell and disabled say a lot about what our nation thinks of the vulnerable. To characterize an assisted living facility as a petri dish reveals how we see the elderly and the weak. Bacteria are generally things we want to be rid of.

After making sure I did not break the zipper on my small carry-on, I noticed I was missing my Egungun elekes. Though a simple multicolored beaded necklace, representing the energy of my African ancestors, it has made me aware of the wisdoms in being connected to your roots. As a descendant of these people in the United States, it is crucial I allow their knowledge to shield me. They were on my ancestral altar, where I always keep them. Over the years, I have learned that going home means to commune with ancestors, and this time I was sure they would reveal themselves and impart knowledge.

The first evening home I sat with my mother watching reruns of *Family Feud*, and she asked me if I would take on the task of writing Uncle Mathes's obituary. She brought me a few from her room as examples and told me which ones she preferred. We contemplated what details to include. After saying goodnight, I sat staring at the screen thinking, What responsibilities come with writing a Black man's life story? Ensuring he was remembered for his *life* rather than his death weighed heavily on me.

I have always struggled to write at night. It is probably because my brothers and I had to wake up early to complete our outdoor chores. I learned to associate the morning with work and the evening with rest. But my time was limited. So I sat at the kitchen table a little longer, my usual writing space. I stacked the heavy three-ring photo albums and curated the photos that best storied the pivotal moments from his life. From the black-and-white first hospital photograph, a sepia family portrait taken in Inkster before their move to Ecorse, a couple of pictures of him from the days when cats from Detroit belonged to the Errol Flynns (flamboyant street gangsters whose hand moves inspired early hip-hop culture and dance), a cap-and-gown photo, one of him dressed to the nines dancing at a family function, a few of him surrounded by next of kin and friends of the family. Emanating from each picture was the jubilation that gave him nicknames such as Floyd-Joy or Pretty Boy Floyd.

It was three days before the service. The majority of the funeral details were put in place: my eldest cousin and I would emcee; the deacon and pastor from our small Baptist church to which my uncle belonged would present the prayer and eulogy; his friend and fellow choir member would perform a song or two; the tents were acquired for serving homemade pastas, fried chicken, pound cakes, and duplex cookies (known as my uncle's favorite dessert); and my first cousins from out of town had just arrived.

Every time my mother came to check on my progress, she could not help but smile. I asked her, "What would you like to say to Uncle Mathes?" She sat down on the bench next to me as if she knew it was time to reconcile with his absence. Before she could finish her thoughts, a wave of simultaneous sadness came over us. We have never refrained from being vulnerable with each other, even as I have grown into a man. I could always count on her as someone who is willing to sit with me in the muddiness of life. We held each other for a moment, the first time since I had arrived home. It was an embrace that we have come accustomed to and one needed to move forward.

My mother requested we all wear white, fitting for a memorial in a time of darkness and appropriate for one taking place outdoors in the heat and humidity of a Michigan summer. The spiritual practice of being in all white breaks from the Western Christian norms we were all raised to follow. My mother had diverted from this practice of wearing black after the murder of her and Uncle Mathes's baby brother Myron (who also lived with us) and the untimely passing of their sister Vernadene and brother Maurice. This was her way of reclaiming mourning from European traditions of lamentation, which have erased Black ways of communing and commemorating the dead, and that reproduce the material conditions that subject Black people to an early grave.

Tents were erected and lawn chairs were arranged six feet apart on the cement basketball court my paternal grandfather poured for us before he passed in 2005. The winds were strong and kept blowing down the easel that displayed photos from the obituary. This was a good sign, because it meant that Oya, the orisha of death and rebirth, had come to bless us. Uncle Mathes's homegoing began and ended with joy and laughter. In between was the shedding of collective tears. Pouring out from our love for him and the care we have for each other.

I watched my two younger brothers cry. The narrative that Black men are afraid of showing their emotions is complex. I imagine the practice of composure and toughness came out of the survival of years of torture, submission, and dispossession. On the other hand, my father taught us never to be afraid of our emotions, especially with one another, because we are all we have.

When my father speaks in sorrow, we all tend to listen. In his usual cowboy attire, he told a story of the complexities of a Black man taking care of his wife's brother, whom he also knew from childhood. According to my father, my Uncle Mathes was a handsome, intelligent, and amiable brother. With sincere honesty, he explained how my uncle's life took an unexpected turn when he was given a mind-altering drug. This made him one of many in his community who never found his way back.

While Uncle Mathes's body and mind sometimes behaved as though he were a youth, my father reminded us that his spirit had matured. In the basement, where he spent a lot of his time lifting weights and jamming to Detroit Black radio, my father consistently witnessed him on his knees praying, with his hands folded, for peace, forgiveness, and protection. Uncle Mathes may have lost his body and mind to the cruelty of this world, but he never ceased to lose faith in himself and God.

This seemed to elevate our collective mourning. Seemed to free us from the burdens we were carrying, because we knew that like

Uncle Mathes we could give them to God, Spirit, and the Universe. It gave us a sense of what it might mean to sincerely answer the questions, *Are you sure you want to be well? Are we ready to carry that weight?*[1]

Remembrance. Mathes Ivory Cross loved riding bikes. All types of bikes, from stationary exercise bikes to road bikes. It was his physical activity, hobby, and transportation. As a youth, I witnessed him riding for miles, all day and into the night. My mother, his younger sister by sixteen months, told me that when they were young, he stole her bike, hitched it to the front of a bus, and rode it to Windsor, Canada. She laughs every time she tells that story.

She explained to me that his relationship with bikes grew from his inability to pass a road test. Although he scored high enough on the multiple-choice written portion, his cognitive disability, induced by a laced cigarette when he was about nineteen years old, altered his capacity to live independently.

After my maternal grandfather passed, he moved from Ecorse, Michigan, a downriver town, to live with us in the country. With zero access to public transit and partial access to my father's barrage of tools and hardware, Uncle Mathes taught himself how to build bikes from scratch and repair them too.

A few summers ago, when I came home from graduate school in Minnesota, I found my vintage Schwinn bike fragmented, a wheel here, the handle bars there, and the brakes nowhere to be found. He had taken the parts from my bike and used them to rebuild his own. Though extremely upset that I would have to search and buy vintage parts, I could not be mad for long, because he was doing what made him happy. Bikes seem to give him a sense of joy, social life, and the freedom of mobility.

However, he preferred to be behind the wheel of a car.

Like a student, he always carried a backpack. In his backpack

---

1. This is a reference to one of my favorite books about healing, *The Salt Eaters* by Toni Cade Bambara.

you would be sure to find a Bible and a driver's training manual. Inspired by my folks who had gotten a new Ford F-150, he convinced a neighbor to sell him their used Pontiac. He was caught joy riding by my younger brother and drove for only a few hours before crashing his new ride.

This was just a couple of years ago before being diagnosed with a rare neurological disease that gradually affected his ability to eat, talk, and walk. He had trouble coming to terms with the fact that we were holding his bikes hostage. When he was able to get a hold of a bike, he would ride despite not possessing the strength and balance to pedal.

He was raised by Black migrants from Mississippi and Louisiana, in a community marked by the perils of the urban crisis: white and Black flight, disinvestment, and one of the most brutal uprisings and youth rebellions ever to be experienced in an American city. Automated like factory labor, the Detroit Metro area and other predominantly urban and Black spaces were reassembled into a staging ground for the War on Drugs. Uncle Mathes and his friends struggled to escape the criminalization of Black youth. It could be argued that he and his peers were some of the first to experience what we now call the school-prison nexus, where experiences in programs like special education limit and steal the life chances and mobility of Black boys, beginning at the age of six. Although he was never incarcerated, the dispossession of intellectual, emotional, and social development impacted his ability to move freely.

After we filled our stomachs, we played spades and whist, listened to music, and even danced into the night. Homegoings are meant to be celebrations of life rather than a gathering of hopelessness and melancholy. We allowed our bodies to be in collaboration. In our collective movement forward, we removed what weighs us down by reclaiming who lifts us up. As a reunion of ancestors, elders, adults, and children, we looked to the past to make sense of our present by retelling where we have been, where we are, and where we plan to go. Despite personal struggles and societal crisis, we gave space for healing ourselves and our community.

Unsure when the mourning would be over, we leaned on the knowledge passed down from our foremothers and fathers who incorporated paths toward love and recovery in spite of being torn and disintegrated. That night we were reminded to follow that path with assurance and wisdom.

FOUR GENIES

Ricardo Levins Morales

"We're all in this together." That was the call echoing in the public square, spoken by activists, health care workers, and politicians alike as the initial shock waves of the pandemic rippled through the social bedrock. But are we? While we're certainly all in this, "together" might be a bit of an overstatement. Our lives are being impacted in ways as different as the chasms of race, class, gender, colonial status, and all the other disease vectors of injustice can make them. Crisis under capitalism is the great amplifier, not the great equalizer.

Since I first wrote those words, in the early days of the pandemic, the shocks have continued. On my birthday this year George Floyd was murdered—center stage, lights up—igniting a firestorm of protest and rebellion that spread across the land, eerily reflected in the burning forests to the west. While images of cops taking a knee circulated in the media, the police system as a whole went on the attack, beating, tear-gassing, arresting. Déjà vu, right? When my family brought me from Puerto Rico as a boy, smoke filled the skies over Chicago in the long, hot summer of 1967. Soon I'd be protesting other police murders—Manuel Ramos, Fred Hampton, Mark Clark. Embarking on what would be a life in what we like to call "the struggle."

But this time it's also different. Like a sapling and the tree it grows into are the same—and also different. The United States back then had not yet reached the peak of its global economic and military power. Today those glory days are long past. The myths that once assured the people's loyalty have toppled one by one along with the monuments to Lee, Calhoun, and Columbus. Police departments frantically hand out ice cream to kids while purchasing drones and noise cannons. The voices in the streets demand that they be gone. The unfinished business of abolition.

As the machines of capital devour forests, and wetlands, grinding up roots and bones and feathers and spitting them out as stock options and financial instruments, the tiny inhabitants of the wild move into our villages. Joining our company with names like zika and ebola and Covid they strike along the vectors of oppression and vulnerability the system provides. Farm workers imprisoned in open fields, billionaires multiplying their profits.

Sheltering in place, therefore, can have different meanings: quality time with parents; confinement with an abusive person; adapting to remote teaching; binge-watching shows; fear of deportation; rest and creativity; separation from loved ones; or grieving loved ones from afar. Many thousands around the country also do not have functional WiFi or cell phone access. And then there are those among us venturing out to work with inadequate protections and with constant worries about what you might unintentionally bring home.

As we rise to this crisis—whether by sheltering and self-care, mutual aid initiatives, wildcat strikes, information sharing, or creative protest—the tectonic plates of our social world are shifting. The old "normal" is damaged beyond repair. Amid the chaos truths long hidden are escaping, like the magic genies of Arab folklore trapped for centuries inside of oil lamps, yearning to be free.

First of these truths is the centrality of working people. Suddenly, packagers and cooks and drivers and nurses and childcare workers, personal care attendants and fast food workers were being praised as "heroes." The very people whose supposed insignificance has long been the justification for low wages and shoddy treatment. Their demands for safety protocols, paid sick leave, health coverage, and corporate closings have resonated widely and have won significant concessions. CEOs and billionaires, on the other hand, could all disappear and no one would notice.

Well, that's not quite true. They've been making such loud smacking noises as they gorge themselves from the public treasury. At the same time they cry out for rollbacks of pollution, labor, and food-safety protections and demand that their workers return immediately—no matter the cost—to the sacred task of producing profit.

Next comes the genie of collective effort. Millions of people are participating in a massive effort in which no one person's actions can make the difference alone but our combined actions can change the course of events. This undermines the learned hopelessness that tells us each that my voice, my protests, my vote, my choices don't matter. Masses pouring into streets in cities and towns proclaiming that Black Lives do Matter. That we are connected. An injury to one is, indeed, an injury to all. "Justice and humanity are often overpowered," Frederick Douglass once observed. "But they are persistent and eternal forces—and fearful to contend against."

The third genie tells us that the resources we've needed were there all along. Trillions of dollars—that were never offered to house, clothe, feed, and heal us—appear out of thin air when the survival of the aristocracy is threatened. The third genie asks, Why is access to all our basic needs controlled by predators, anyway? Why not by us?

Last but not least comes the biggest and most frightening genie of them all: the clear evidence that generosity, sharing, and solidarity are better organizing principles than greed. Even the mighty corporate elite—that worships greed and preys on the vulnerable—as a desperate measure had to resort to a strategy of sharing resources just to save itself, its leaders terrified that the idea might catch on.

I take my place with the artists, drummers, dancers and healers, the poets and the elders. Our task is, as always, to make the invisible visible and make the visible feel manageable. For me that involves working with my solid team of coworkers out of a storefront studio in South Minneapolis, sending messages into the world and supporting whatever hands-on organizing we can. The people tell us what they need. Children need animals to color. Teachers need stories of resilience. Organizers need models of resistance.

Our enemies also tell us how to resist them. If fear, confusion, and despair are their weapons, then hope and clarity must be our medicines. If they depend on a parched landscape of isolation and division, then we offer the quenching waters of connection and unity. It's difficult, for sure, but not complicated. Mutual aid and labor activism are necessary to win the things our people need. Drumming, song, and art are to remind them of who they are.

We will get through this. I mean the collective *we*, because not all of us will make it. Our hearts ache for those already in mourning. There will be more losses to come. Still, our people will survive. But this time we will have four genies to help us in our work. Four genies that are not about to be crammed back into those little lamps. In fact, it's not too early to start planning—for when all of us getting together is a thing again—a big ole lamp-smashing party.

ALL THE STARS AFLAME

Shannon Gibney

I wrote this during what many of us experienced as a Siege on South Minneapolis by white supremacists, following the widespread protests here against the murder of George Floyd. I remember it as a raw, open time, in which we struggled for some semblance of safety and meaning while surviving and trying to live in the city we love. Apart from organizing with my neighbors, the deepest thing that connected me at that time was the knowledge that I am just one in a long, long line of Black folks who resisted and told the stories that needed to be told in the times when they might otherwise be lost, forgotten, or not spoken at all. And that truth buoyed me beyond and amidst all of it, giving me space and place to rest in our tradition.

I always go back to Baldwin.

"Try to imagine how you would feel if you woke up one morning to find the sun shining and all the stars aflame. You would be frightened because it is out of the order of nature. Any upheaval in the universe is terrifying because it so profoundly attacks one's sense of one's own reality. Well, the black man has functioned in the white man's world as a fixed star, as an immovable pillar: and as he moves out of his place, heaven and earth are shaken to their foundation."

This quote is from *The Fire Next Time,* James Baldwin's seminal collection of essays on race, power, and politics. It was published in 1962, but might as well have been written yesterday. Baldwin's prescient observations about the psychology of American racism have always felt like a revelation to me—a voice from the grave whispering earth-shattering truths in my ear that should have been obvious. Even after sixty years, Baldwin's words still manage somehow to occupy the present tense. To have effectively described the roots of white denial and disbelief that not only black people—but much of the nation, including black, brown, indigenous, and even some white folks—are just DONE with the American police state and its relentless destruction of black bodies. . . . That is something else. That is divination.

The white hand-wringing. What can we do? The images circulating everywhere, more popping up every day, fresh evidence of police abuse against protesters. The growing number of injured or even killed. The carnage of burning buildings and broken windows. And the reliable echoes of that ever-loved rhetorical question: But why would they bring such destruction to their own communities? The reclamation of the "bad apple" argument. The violent white nationalists (who always manage to be both well organized and a complete shock to their fellow white folks' sense of reality) infiltrating protests and communities in Minneapolis and beyond, holding rallies in our parks and attempting to burn down libraries and minority-owned businesses. Our political leadership's profound inability to understand the violence that is unfolding, that has always been with us but that hasn't had a wellspring big enough from which to burst up till now. Their shock at watching civil society collapse so quickly. The disbelief that this is happening on top of another crisis: Covid-19. The insistence that this virus is more deadly than racism, so protest is a public health hazard. The many past failed attempts at reforming the seemingly intractable police state. The chanting, growing louder and louder, I Can't Breathe! I Can't Breathe!

All of these are Baldwin's stars aflame. Jamar Clark. Philando Castile. George Floyd. All those ghosts. All those black bodies that were heretofore immovable pillars are now on the move. They walk among us, and we among them, the living merging with the dead. They will have their day. They will be heard. And their voices are what is shaking heaven and earth to their foundation.

HUMILITY, SINCERITY, BANANA OIL

Louise Erdrich

PAT GOURNEAU'S FIGHT AGAINST TERMINATION

TURTLE MOUNTAIN CONSOLIDATED AGENCY NEWS LETTER

× × ×

Vol. III • Belcourt, North Dakota
February 1954 • Issue II

× × ×

The dates for the hearings on the Turtle Mountain termination bill have been set for March 2 and 3, 1954, and a delegation has been authorized to be present for these hearings in Washington D.C. It would be to our advantage to be there to state our views on this issue which is of great importance to every enrolled member of the Turtle Mountain Band of Chippewa.

We have no funds to finance this delegation and at the regular meeting of the Advisory Committee held February 1, 1954, various means of raising money were discussed. As a result, a boxing card has been arranged between the local boys and those from Bottineau. This should be a good one and a treat for fight fans.

The date scheduled for this event is Saturday, February 20 at 7:30 p.m.

The entire proceeds from this show will be used to finance our delegation to Washington to protest the bill. You are all urged to attend. It is doubtful whether the proceeds will be sufficient to meet the expenses of the trip so it may be necessary, as a last resort, to canvass the reservation asking for individual donations in whatever amount you can afford. IF THIS IS NECESSARY, GIVE WHAT YOU CAN.

✖ ✖ ✖

THOUGHT FOR THE DAY

The average man is proof that the average woman can take a joke.

✖ ✖ ✖

My grandfather, Patrick Gourneau, wrote a Tribal Chairman's Corner column in the community newsletter and was responsible for the jokes. He served as chairman of the Turtle Mountain Advisory Committee during the crisis year when our tribe was nearly terminated. House Concurrent Resolution 108 was passed in July 1953. The proposed bill aimed to declare null all treaties made with American Indians, and in that way to "free" all tribal people from health and education services guaranteed in those treaties for as long as the grass shall grow and the rivers flow. Thirteen tribes including ours were deemed immediately ready for what the authors of the resolution termed *emancipation*. The news of the bill came to most tribal leaders in a scattershot way, usually via area newspapers. An official government announcement did not arrive until late September.

The salary for my grandfather's chairman job, which became more than full time, was thirty dollars per month. When the tribe's existence was jeopardized, Pat Gourneau refused to take any salary at all. He and my grandmother Mary had fed and supported their family through the Depression by working Pat's allotment into a model truck garden. They still gardened, but now Pat also worked as a night watchman in the Turtle Mountain Jewel Bearing Plant. He drove his beloved Nash Ambassador over uncertain roads to the modern one-story building in the off-reservation town Rolla, where jewel bearings used in ordnance and in Bulova watches were manufactured.

In a letter to my parents, Grandpa Pat noted punching 4 a.m. on the watchman's clock. He used his days to muster support to fight termination. He wrote letters to government officials and newspaper columnists, met with tribal members, and strategized with an attorney, John A. Stormon, from Rolla. In the entire previous week, Grandpa Pat had slept a total of twelve hours. He was beyond tired. To keep himself awake, he wrote letters to his children. A letter to my parents included this description: "Every now and then, I'd jerk my head out of a nod and darn if I wouldn't see a little boy sitting on the band saw here in the shop. After my head would clear a bit what was the little boy had turned out to be the motor on the band saw. It happened time after time." The day before, he had nodded off eating his breakfast sandwiches and jerked awake to see he'd dropped one. "I bent my head," he wrote, "and asked the one on the floor, 'How did *you* get down there?'" He spoke of resolving to get more sleep from then on and noted that "the proposed Bill is just about the worst thing to come out of Washington for the people of this reservation." The letter was dated October 9, 1953.

Ten days later he was down in Fargo with the Advisory Committee and other tribal members, meeting with BIA Area Director John M. Cooper, who read the draft of the Termination Bill aloud and attempted to explain each section. The first tribal member to comment, Mr. Alex Martin, asked that the bill be explained in more common language and the shortest way possible. Mr. Graham Holmes, Area Counsel for the BIA, tried to clarify:

> Simply, once and for all, it provides that there won't be any more Indian Service for Turtle Mountain. There won't be any more trust land and the Indians will be just exactly like the whites as far as the government is concerned.

The first to grasp the meaning of the bill was Mrs. Toby Martin, who said that the bill did not suit her or her people because nobody would be able to afford to send their children to school, or go to the hospital. But there was confusion—many of the tribal members spoke little or no English. Mr. Summer's testimony was translated from Chippewa (Anishinaabe) by Louie St. Claire:

> It makes me mad that I cannot understand. I am sorry that I cannot understand. Are they just going to drop us like that . . . . Do you see any rich persons here? I don't know of anyone. I got a few cents in my pocket, that is all I have got . . . . Ever since the white man came in 1492 they started robbing the Indian of his riches. Every since the white man has been making money and is rich, that is why they have it easy to pay taxes.

"We don't want to have anything to do with this bill. We are going to fight it down. That is how it stands," said Francis Poitra.

Mrs. Peter Oneside said she was "sorry you did not have any one to interpret. There are many people back here that don't know what is being said."

Pat Gourneau took a vote on the question, which he phrased: "Do you want to dispense with the services of the U.S. Government on this reservation?"

Yes—0   No—47

My parents lived then where they do now, in Wahpeton, an hour south of Fargo. After the meeting Pat drove down to visit them in their small apartment on the top floor of a BIA house. My mother was newly pregnant. With me, it turned out. She snapped a photograph of her father carrying the same briefcase that he would lug to Washington, D.C., come March. A day after the visit, he was back in Belcourt, filing a petition signed by hundreds of tribal members, to oppose the bill. A week after filing the petition, he was celebrating Bulova Day. He described meeting the governor and other notables. He also mentioned meeting "Old Grand Dad, Hiram Walker, and the Four Rosies," whose company he passed up. Pat had long ago stopped drinking, though he still smoked his favorite cigars, Stetsons. After a celebratory dinner, Pat put on his regalia, including beadwork made by his cousin Virginia Iron Bear. He danced traditional style on the high school gym stage for General Omar Bradley and Mr. Bulova himself, whom he nicknamed Chief Prince of Time.

The Termination Bill, an ongoing catastrophe for the tribes who suffered its imposition, was authored by Utah Senator Arthur Vivian Watkins, the chairman of the Senate Committee on Indian Affairs. Watkins was also a Mormon. He wrote:

The more I go into this Indian problem the more I am convinced that we have made some terrible mistakes in the past. It seems to me that the time has come for us to correct some of these mistakes and help the Indians stand on their own two feet and become a white and delightsome people as the Book of Mormon prophesied they would become. Of course, I realize that the Gospel of Jesus Christ will be the motivating factor, but it is difficult to teach the Gospel when they don't understand the English language and have had no training in caring for themselves. The Gospel should be a great stimulus and I am longing and praying for the time when the Indians will accept it in overwhelming numbers.

The Turtle Mountain Band of Chippewa, a sovereign nation, was at the time worth less than five hundred thousand dollars—most of that in land holdings. Tribal Judge was a position that was unpaid except for a portion of fines that the judge imposed.

Total fines for the year came to $69.74. The tribe held the benefit boxing match and passed the hat among its impoverished citizens, in order to send representatives to Washington to argue for its continued existence. But they were lucky. Other tribes like the Southern Paiute were unable to raise money to send delegations. They were terminated. The Menominee and Klamath were terminated. Over a hundred tribes were eventually terminated. But when the Turtle Mountain Chippewa argued against, resisted, and won their case against termination, their example fortified other tribes to fight harder.

Replacing the word *emancipation* with the word *termination* was one of the first methods of attack. Replacing the word *freedom* with *no government services* was another way of fending off doublespeak.

Reading over the government publishing office transcript of the joint hearing on their case, March 2 and 3, 1953, I'm overcome by the magnitude of what the Turtle Mountain delegation—Edward (Chick) Jollie, Leo Jeanotte, and Pat Gourneau—faced once they arrived at our nation's capital. First, they threaded through a state of emergency. Washington, D.C. was filled with wailing sirens and uniformed officers. Shots had been fired in the vicinity of the capitol building.

Not only was Grandpa sleepless and anxious, but he had injured his hand and was told that his splinted finger might have to be amputated. They were facing a congressional committee completely hostile to their existence as American Indians. When, at last, my grandfather was allowed to deliver his statement, Senator Arthur V. Watkins barely seemed to listen. He interrupted Pat Gourneau several times to preach about his values. Watkins had the gall to say, "In my area, the whites got the poor land in the reservation."

Got the poor land in the reservation? You mean the allotments bought on the cheap or tax forfeited after the rest of Utah was stolen? He goes on to say that was okay because "within a year the Indians leased all of their land. They just didn't want to farm. That is true today . . . I seriously doubt that Indians like to farm."

He was talking to a master farmer. Photographs of Pat Gourneau's truck garden are in the State Historical and National Archives. His beautiful rolling fields of corn and stands of rhubarb, pumpkins, squash, and hills of potatoes were the pride of the reservation. And he was not the only farmer. The wonderfully named Telesphore Renault, last signer of the petition opposing termination, raised champion pigs in a round barn between Belcourt and Dunseith. Gardens were survival. Many people in the Turtle Mountains had at least a kitchen garden or grew their own potatoes and squash, kept chickens, or raised a cow.

"What little tillable land we have on the reservation is farmed by Indian farmers," said my grandfather.

Senator Watkins then attempted to lecture my grandfather, who kept sliding out from under each attempt, determined to press on with his main points: the people are impoverished, relocation is not the answer, the Turtle Mountain question should be treated as a special problem, the opposition to termination is strong and unanimous.

Watkins, oblivious, patronizing, says, "After all, the Government can't solve your problems for you. Most of them have to be solved by yourselves . . . . There would be nothing permanently cured there that you don't cure yourself. No government, no matter how benevolent, can put ambition into people. That has to be developed by themselves. You can't legislate morality, character, or any of those fine virtues into people.

"You have to walk by walking," concludes the senator, addressing a delegation of people who grew up without another means of transportation. People who were, perhaps, the walkingest walkers in North America.

Pat ignores the senator. He talks about how the tribe must be consulted in any decisions about its future destiny. I can hear his voice raised here, him talking quickly, firmly, trying not to give Watkins the chance to grandstand. However, he must have paused to take a breath, because after a few paragraphs Watkins did what he did with each Indian delegate. He went personal. He asked if Pat Gourneau, hard working all of his life, *if* he had a job. Then Watkins questioned him closely on blood quantum. There was no right answer to these questions.

Watkins used any answer to belittle, humiliate, and then to lecture. David Delorme, a John Jay scholar at the University of Texas, and a tribal member, got this treatment from Watkins. Delorme testified eloquently, hitting the same points as the other speakers. He set out a scenario of the extreme poverty of a tribe situated on an inadequate land base. He mentioned absolute opposition to termination. Then hammered away on how much more federal money would be needed to train people in order to enter the national workforce. North Dakota Senator Milton R. Young insisted that this had to be a whole lot of money. He referred to the newspaper articles by Pat Gourneau's friend, Minot columnist Bob Cory, which painted a detailed picture of the economic struggles of the tribe. The possibility of relocating the entire tribe was raised.

Relocate from his farm, his cornfields, and prized stands of rhubarb? The beds of moss roses he grew just for their beauty? My grandfather must have swallowed hard.

Arthur Watkins was a righteous man with no sense of humor and a zealot's narcissism. Patrick Gourneau was a loving realist who treasured jokes, delighted in children's remarks, found irony in even the grimmest situation. Watkins was the most powerful senator of his era and made the cover of *Time* magazine that same year. Pat Gourneau had at best an eighth-grade government boarding school education, but he was a devoted autodidact and read every book his children brought home from school. They were opposites in most respects, but they were also alike in one vital regard. Both had an innate sense of deportment and valued civility. Both were polite (unless Watkins was questioning a witness) and both appreciated politeness in others.

Perhaps the most telling detail in the entire aftermath of the testimony appears in a handwritten paragraph that my grandfather added to an onionskin copy of a letter. Written to Senator Milton R. Young barely a week after he returned from Washington, D.C., this was a thank-you letter. At least, one paragraph was a thank-you. The rest of the letter detailed second thoughts that my grandfather had on one of Watkins's obsessions, blood quantum:

> The government . . . recognized and negotiated with them as Indians of an identifiable group irrespective of degree of Indian blood. To disclaim us now on account of the degree of Indian blood factor would be an abrogation of an agreement . . . . the Government should assume full responsibility to bring about corrective measures. Not by a hastily drawn bill as admitted at the hearings, but by a good comprehensive and constructive program, one that would prove a blessing instead of a boomerang.

At the end of the copy of his letter, in a note written only to my parents, Grandpa Pat said that Committee Senator Watkins "did considerable harping on the degree of Indian blood factor. Hence this letter to Senator Young." Which was ostensibly a thank-you letter. Pat goes on to say that Senator Young was a swell guy, that he had worked on him all summer, and that the work had sure paid off:

You have no idea how belligerent some of those old Senators on a Committee can get. Senator Watkins simply enjoys tearing a witness apart and so does Harrison of Wyoming.

I have read my grandfather's letters over and over for at least thirty years. They are difficult to read because he lost his nimble brain and complex language incrementally to atherosclerosis. His slow deterioration is hard to think of when contrasted with the lively storytelling in his writing. Still, I look to the letters, wondering, How did he do it? What was there about this man that made him, in a word, a great man to his people? What gifts did he call on to build a wide coalition of friends, what qualities made him an ambassador of good will, and how did he win this lopsided fight? One key to his strategy lies in this paragraph:

> I went to the hearings with a plan and laid it before our members in Congress for their inspection. It had their full approval. It was very simple and very humble and seasoned with a little banana oil. . . .

Pat's strategy—simplicity, humility, banana oil. Here is how he eventually disarmed Senator Watkins:

> After my statement . . . the meeting recessed. I immediately went down to Senator Watkins's office and expressed my deepest appreciation for the courteous way he treated me. (As I just said, he wasn't courteous at all.) It developed that I was the first and only person to do this during all of the hearings. All of our witnesses were well treated after that. Most witnesses were ripped to pieces on other tribes' hearings.

I still feel that it is dismally unfair that my grandfather, and not Arthur Watkins, suffered from the tremendous stress of their encounter. On the way home from Washington, D.C., my grandfather was afflicted by the first of what turned out to be many strokes. Still, he kept his job and he worked on bettering the reservation school system. He worked on a new tribal constitution, and he took on many smaller tribal matters that occasionally surface in his writing.

In several of his letters, my grandfather writes about the problems of distributing the huge semi-loads of butter that were, it seems, delivered more—everybody has a nickname. Often people took a butter distribution for their given name, and another was signed out under a nickname. It was hard to make a fair accounting of the distribution. Pat writes that it took a day and a half to trace duplicate butter issues, and he writes of those who took butter under false pretenses: "Crooked Injuns like that should deserve a good slapping around with House Concurrent Resolution 108."

But it was my grandfather who got slapped around by that bill. His terror and concern for his people, the grueling work of parsing out strategy and building coalitions involved in fighting termination, and the need to provide for his family were so overwhelming that he just stopped sleeping more than two or three hours. And his finger wouldn't heal. It was still in a splint. Once he returned to the reservation he kept up the letters to my parents, apologizing for his handwriting. He was on antibiotics for the first time in his life. In one letter, he swears that he saw "the little penicillins and streptomycins knocking each other over to get at the bacteria. One big strapping streptomycin grabbed a little virus and just hugged it to death." He also says that his finger really might have to be amputated now, but that he'll "still use it for emphasis, to make short points."

The short point is this. In a lopsided fight, throw everything at your opponent. In Pat's fight he threw senators, newspaper columnists, local lawyers, petitions, scholars, tribal opposition, humility, sincerity, and banana oil. The Turtle Mountain Band of Chippewa was not terminated. And although he began to lose his health, Pat continued on as chairman until the tribe was out of debt. He danced at every powwow he could get to, including one at the Seattle World's Fair, attended the Belcourt High School Prom and kicked up his heels in 1970, and in 1972 my high school graduation in Wahpeton. Pat Gourneau appeared on North Dakota travel brochures and was often asked by the state of North Dakota to name visiting dignitaries. Even as he fought to maintain his hold on cognition, there were flashes of his signature humor. When Tricia Nixon arrived in Fargo, my grandfather was driven down to greet her and to bestow upon her a traditional Indian name. He told me that he gave her a name that sounded nice in the Ojibwe language. I asked him what the name meant.

He answered, deadpan, "Woman Getting Off An Airplane."

It was a joke—he would never have misused his gift. I learned later that he'd really given her a beautiful name that was more like a bird alighting. But for a while I cherished the irreverent thought that his name for Tricia Nixon was another instance of banana oil, perfectly applied.

ACKNOWLEDGMENTS

First I want to thank Michael Kiesow Moore for inviting me and members of Twin Cities Black Women Writing to read at his series in 2014. An audience member's comment was the impetus for my starting More Than a Single Story. I thank the Loft Literary Center, especially Bao Phi and Sherrie Fernandez-Williams, for supporting our initial idea and for their continued support. Also Dillon Young and Kia Vang at Hennepin Libraries, Alayne Hopkins and Wendy Werdin at the Friends of the Saint Paul Libraries, Barbara Lund and Sonja Ausen at Wisdom Ways Center for Spirituality, and Paul Lai at Ramsey County Library. Thanks to all of the 119 writers and arts activists who participated during the first five years of our programs, and the countless numbers of people who have taken the time to participate as audience members. Many thanks to the voters of Minnesota, the Metropolitan Regional Arts Council, the Minnesota State Arts Board, the Minneapolis Foundation Fund for Safe Communities, and the Transformative Black Led Movement Fund. Special thanks to dear friend and colleague David Mura for saying yes, to all the writers who lent their words to this effort, and to editor extraordinaire Erik Anderson and the staff at the University of Minnesota Press. To the amazing and energetic people who keep More Than a Single Story going: Sandy Moore, Makayla Overton, John Thew, and my amazing granddaughters Tess Montgomery and Nia Davis. I couldn't have done any of this without the loving support of my family and my ancestors who continue to guide me.

—Carolyn Holbrook

I'd like to thank Carolyn Holbrook for asking me to coedit this anthology and for inviting me to facilitate panels for More Than a Single Story on issues facing men of color. She's been a longtime friend and colleague; together we've seen the community of writers of color in Minnesota grow and flourish, and she's done so much over the years to make that happen. Erik Anderson, our editor at the University of Minnesota Press, has been such an enthusiastic supporter of this project, and his judgments, insights, and passion have been absolutely instrumental to this anthology. The staff at the University of Minnesota Press have also been so supportive and a pleasure to work with. I thank each and every one of the writers in this book: they make me proud to be part of this fabulous literary community, and the excellence, diversity, and range of their work still astonish me. I'd like to thank particularly Alexs Pate, Bao Phi, Ed Bok Lee, and Sun Yung Shin for their support of me and my work. Finally, I thank my wife, Susan Sencer, and my children, Samantha, Nikko, and Tomo, for their love and for making room and giving support for the work I do.

—David Mura

CONTRIBUTORS

Suleiman Adan is a writer, educator, and grassroots organizer in the Twin Cities. He works as a program manager with Reading and Math Inc. and is also a Quran/Arabic and Islamic studies teacher at the Northwest Islamic Community Center in Plymouth, Minnesota. He is a project manager and board chair for the Global Alliance of Muslims for Equality, an international NGO.

Pamela R. Fletcher Bush works as a writer, an editor, and the CEO and publisher of Arcata Press | Saint Paul Almanac. She is professor emerita of English at St. Catherine University in St. Paul, Minnesota, and coeditor of *Blues Vision: African American Writing from Minnesota*; *As We See It: A Fresh Look at Vision Loss*; and *Transforming a Rape Culture*.

Mary Moore Easter received an Artist Initiative Grant from the Minnesota State Arts Board and is the author of four poetry books: *Free Papers: Inspired by the Testimony of Eliza Winston, a Mississippi Slave Escaped to Freedom in Minnesota in 1860*; *The Body of the World*, finalist for the Minnesota Book Award in Poetry; *Walking from Origins*; and *From the Flutes of Our Bones*. She is founder and director of the dance program at Carleton College and has a long career in Minnesota as an independent dancer and choreographer. Her poems have been published in *Poetry*, *Water~Stone*, and *Prairie Schooner*. She is a Cave Canem alumni fellow.

Louise Erdrich is the author of seventeen novels as well as volumes of poetry, children's books, short stories, and a memoir of early motherhood. Her novel *The Night Watchman* won the 2021 Pulitzer Prize for fiction. Her novel *The Round House* won the National Book Award for Fiction; *The Plague of Doves* received the Anisfield-Wolf Book Award and was a finalist for the Pulitzer Prize; and her debut novel, *Love Medicine*, was the winner of the National Book Critics Circle Award. She has received the Library of Congress Prize in American Fiction, the PEN/Saul Bellow Award for Achievement in American Fiction, and the Dayton Literary Peace Prize. She lives in Minnesota with her daughters and is the owner of Birchbark Books, a small independent bookstore in Minneapolis.

Anika Fajardo was born in Colombia and raised in Minnesota. She is the author of *Magical Realism for Non-Believers: A Memoir of Finding Family* (Minnesota, 2019) and the middle-grade novels *What If a Fish* and *Meet Me Halfway*. She lives in Minneapolis with her family.

Safy-Hallan Farah is a culture writer from Minneapolis.

Sherrie Fernandez-Williams earned an MFA from Hamline University. She is the author of *Soft: A Memoir*. She has received a Minnesota State Arts Board Artist Initiative Grant, a Beyond the Pure Fellowship, a SASE/Jerome Grant, and is a 2021 Jerome Hill Artist Fellow. She was a Loft Mentor Series winner in Creative Nonfiction and a Jones' Playwright Commission Award Winner, and she was selected for the Givens Black Writers Collaborative. Her poems and essays have been published in literary journals, including *New Limestone Review, Aquifer: The Florida Review*, and *the minnesota review*.

Shannon Gibney is a writer, educator, activist, and author of *See No Color* and *Dream Country*, young adult novels that won Minnesota Book Awards. She is on the faculty in English at Minneapolis College, where she teaches writing. She is a Bush Artist and McKnight Writing Fellow. She coedited, with Kao Kalia Yang, *What God Is*

Honored Here? Writings on Miscarriage and Infant Loss by and for Native Women and Women of Color (Minnesota, 2019), and her latest novel, *Botched,* explores themes of transracial adoption through speculative memoir.

Kathryn Haddad is a writer, teacher, speaker, and community organizer who explores contemporary Arab American experiences and reflects on the political reality of life for Arab and Muslim Americans. She received an Bush Fellowship for her work with the Arab American community; the 2018 Kay Sexton Award from the Minnesota Book Awards; and was a 2019–20 Jerome Fellow in Playwriting. Her plays and creative nonfiction have been published and performed throughout the United States. She cofounded Mizna, one of the few Arab American arts and literary organizations in the United States, and served as its artistic and executive director for twelve years. She is now artistic and executive director of New Arab American Theater Works and teaches high school in Bloomington, Minnesota.

Carolyn Holbrook is founder and director of More Than a Single Story, as well as the founder of SASE: The Write Place. She is a writer, educator, and an advocate for the healing power of the arts. Her essay collection *Tell Me Your Names and I Will Testify* (Minnesota, 2020) received a Minnesota Book Award for Memoir and Creative Nonfiction. She is coauthor of Dr. Josie Johnson's memoir *Hope in the Struggle* (Minnesota, 2019), and her essays have been published widely, in *A Good Time for the Truth: Race in Minnesota* and *Blues Vision: African American Writing from Minnesota,* as well as many other publications. She was the first person of color to win the Kay Sexton Award from the Minnesota Book Awards and the Friends of the St. Paul Public Libraries for contributions to Minnesota literature.

Tish Jones is a poet, educator, cultural strategist, and cultural producer. She is founder and executive director of TruArt Speaks, an arts and culture nonprofit in St. Paul, Minnesota. She has performed poetry throughout the United States, and her work can be found in *A Moment of Silence* (Tru Ruts and the Playwrights' Center) and the Minnesota Humanities Center's anthology *Blues Vision: African American Writing from Minnesota*.

Ezekiel Joubert III is an educator, scholar, and creative writer. He is assistant professor of Educational Foundations in the Division of Advanced and Applied Studies at California State University–Los Angeles. His research and writing focus on the intersections of racial capitalism and Black education, the political economy of student mobility, the history of educational inequality in Black rural communities near Metro Detroit and in the Midwest, and Black organic educational intellectual thought and activism.

Douglas Kearney has published seven collections, including *Sho* and *Buck Studies,* winner of the Theodore Roethke Memorial Poetry Award and the Firecracker Award for Poetry from the Community of Literary Magazines and Presses, and a California Book Award silver medalist in poetry. He has written a collection of libretti, *Someone Took They Tongues,* and his *Mess and Mess and* was a Small Press Distribution Handpicked Selection. His newest collection is *Sho*. His operas include *Sucktion, Mordake, Crescent City, Sweet Land,* and *Comet / Poppea,* commissioned by the American Modern Opera Company. He received a Whiting Writer's Award, a Foundation for Contemporary Arts Cy Twombly Award for Poetry, and residencies and fellowships from Cave Canem and the Rauschenberg Foundation. He teaches creative writing at the University of Minnesota–Twin Cities and lives in St. Paul with his family.

Ed Bok Lee attended kindergarten in Seoul, South Korea, and grew up in North Dakota and Minnesota. He was later educated in South Korea, Kazakhstan, and on the west and east coasts of the United States. He has written three books of poetry: *Real Karaoke People, Whorled,* and *Mitochondrial Night.* Honors for his books include an American Book Award from the Before Columbus Foundation, a PEN Open Book Award, a Minnesota Book Award, and an Asian

American Literary Award (Members' Choice). He teaches fine arts at Metropolitan State University and lives in South Minneapolis.

Ricardo Levins Morales is a Puerto Rican artist and trickster organizer based in Minneapolis. His organizing life began in the Chicago Black Panther Defense Committee and has included the Alliance for Cultural Democracy, the Northland Poster Collective, Labor Notes, the Great Lakes Commons, and most recently MPD150. He supports activists and organizers in the work of healing and liberation.

Arleta Little is a writer and culture worker living and practicing in the Twin Cities. As former director of the Givens Foundation for African American Literature, she studied with Amiri Baraka, Sonia Sanchez, Ishmael Reed, Patricia Smith, Alexs Pate, J. Otis Powell?!, and other definitive writers. Her poetry has been published in *Blues Vision: African American Writing from Minnesota* and in *Konch* magazine. She coauthored *Hope in the Struggle* with civil rights activist and educator Josie Johnson and writer Carolyn Holbrook. She is arts program officer and director of artist fellowships at the McKnight Foundation in Minneapolis.

Resmaa Menakem is a healer, coach, and organizational strategist; founder of the Cultural Somatics Institute (https://culturalsomatics university.thinkific.com/); and author of *My Grandmother's Hands: Racialized Trauma and the Pathway to Mending Our Hearts and Bodies*. Resmaa's work focuses on the healing of trauma; on coaching leaders through civil unrest, organizational change, and community building; and on Somatic Abolitionism (the title of his blog at *Psychology Today*, https://www.psychologytoday.com/us/blog/somatic-abolitionism). To learn more about Resmaa, visit https://www.resmaa.com/.

Tess Montgomery, a North Minneapolis native, is digital marketing specialist at Twin Cities PBS–TPT and marketing coordinator for More Than a Single Story. She has been a Fellow with the Josie R.

Johnson Leadership Academy, a Fellow with New Sector Academy, and a digital production intern with Krista Tippett's *On Being*. She is passionate about the power of grassroots, community-led organizing and believes in the principles of Ubuntu (I am because you are) and Ujima (collective work and responsibility) to build and maintain a strong community. She holds a degree in journalism and mass communications from Drake University.

Ahmad Qais Munhazim is assistant professor of global studies at the Thomas Jefferson University in Philadelphia. As an interdisciplinary scholar and decolonial writer, their work troubles borders of academia, activism, and art while focusing on everyday experiences of migration and war in the lives of queer and trans individuals. Born and raised in Afghanistan and exiled currently in Philadelphia, Munhazim identifies as genderqueer, Muslim, and displaced. They hold a PhD in political science from the University of Minnesota and co-founded Minnesota Caravan of Love, a queer and trans Muslim-led community organizing group in the Twin Cities.

David Mura has written ten books, including the memoirs *Turning Japanese*, a *New York Times* Notable Book; *Where the Body Meets Memory*; and four poetry collections, *After We Lost Our Way*, a National Poetry Contest winner; *The Colors of Desire*, which received the Carl Sandburg Award; *Angels for the Burning*; *The Last Incantations*; and *A Stranger's Journey: Race, Identity, and Narrative Craft in Writing*. He teaches at VONA, a writers' conference for writers of color, and has worked with Alexs Pate's Innocent Classroom, a program designed to improve relationships between teachers and students of color.

Melissa Olson is an Indigenous person of mixed Anishinaabe and Euro-American heritage, a tribal citizen of the Leech Lake Band of Ojibwe. For several years, Melissa has worked as a writer and producer of independent public media serving as the co–managing editor of the MinneCulture program at KFAI Fresh Air Community Radio in Minneapolis. Melissa lives in Minneapolis.

Alexs Pate is president and CEO of Innocent Technologies and the creator of the Innocent Classroom. He has written five novels, a children's book, and a work of nonfiction, and he has curated several literary anthologies. His latest book is *The Innocent Classroom: Dismantling Racial Bias for Children of Color.*

Bao Phi is a Vietnamese American Minnesotan, born in Vietnam and raised in the Phillips neighborhood of South Minneapolis. He is a spoken word artist, a poet, a children's book author, a community member, a nonprofit arts administrator, a refugee, and a father.

Mona Susan Power is the author of three books of fiction, *The Grass Dancer, Roofwalker,* and *Sacred Wilderness.* Her first novel was awarded the PEN/Hemingway Prize. Her short fiction and essays have been published in journals, magazines, and anthologies, including *The Best American Short Stories, Atlantic Monthly, Paris Review, Granta, Missouri Review,* and *Ploughshares* (Solos Series). She is an enrolled member of the Standing Rock Sioux tribe and is currently settled in Minnesota.

Marcie Rendon is a citizen of the White Earth Nation. She received a McKnight Distinguished Artist Award and was included on *Oprah Magazine*'s list of thirty-one Native American authors to read in 2020. Her novel *Girl Gone Missing* was nominated at the Edgars for the Sue Grafton Memorial Award of G. P. Putnam's Sons, and *Murder on the Red River* received the Pinckley Women's Debut Crime Novel Award and was a finalist for a Western Writers of America Spur Award.

Samantha Sencer-Mura is a biracial Japanese American woman living in Minneapolis on stolen Dakota land. She is the executive director at 826 MSP, a writing, tutoring, and publishing center for youth with the mission to empower the next generation of Twin Cities authors. She earned a degree in critical theory and social justice from Occidental College and a degree in school leadership from the Harvard Graduate School of Education.

Said Shaiye is a Somali writer who calls Minneapolis home. He is working on his MFA degree at the University of Minnesota, and his debut book *Are You Borg Now?* is forthcoming.

Erin Sharkey is a writer, arts, and abolition organizer, cultural worker, and film producer based in Minneapolis. She has an MFA in creative writing from Hamline University and is the cofounder, with Junauda Petrus, of an experimental arts collective called Free Black Dirt. She is editing *A Darker Wilderness*, a forthcoming anthology of Black nature writing for Milkweed Editions. In 2021, she was awarded the Black Seed Fellowship from Black Visions and the Headwaters Foundation for Justice. She teaches with the Minnesota Prison Writers Workshop.

신 선 영 辛善英 **Sun Yung Shin** is a Korean American poet, editor, children's book author, and writer whose work has been published in *Poetry, Bomb* magazine, and the 2021 Gwangju Biennale, among other venues. Her poetry collections have won an Asian American Literary Award and a Minnesota Book Award. Her edited anthologies include *What We Hunger For: Refugee and Immigrant Writers on Food and Family*; *A Good Time for the Truth: Race in Minnesota*; and *Outsiders Within: Writing on Transracial Adoption* (Minnesota, 2021). Her fourth book of poems, *The Wet Hex,* is forthcoming. With poet Su Hwang she codirects Poetry Asylum in Minneapolis.

Michael Torres was born and brought up in Pomona, California. His first collection, *An Incomplete List of Names,* was a National Poetry Series selection. Visit him at michaeltorreswriter.com.

Diane Wilson is a Dakota writer whose debut novel, *The Seed Keeper,* was recently published. Her memoir *Spirit Car: Journey to a Dakota Past* received a Minnesota Book Award and was selected for the One Minneapolis, One Read program; her nonfiction book *Beloved Child: A Dakota Way of Life* was awarded the Barbara Sudler Award from History Colorado. Her writing has been featured in many publications, including the anthology *A Good Time for the Truth: Race in Minnesota*. She has received a Bush Foundation Fellowship as well as awards from the Minnesota State Arts Board and the Jerome Foundation. She mentors a cohort of emerging Native writers, is a descendant of the Mdewakanton Oyate, and is enrolled on the Rosebud Reservation.

Kao Kalia Yang is a Hmong American writer for both children and adults. Her books have been recognized by the National Endowment for the Arts, the Dayton's Literary Peace Prize, the Chautauqua Institute, the National Book Critics Circle Award, and with four Minnesota Book Awards. She is the Edelstein-Keller Writer in Residence in the creative writing program of the University of Minnesota. Her books include *The Latehomecomer: A Hmong Family Memoir, The Song Poet, The Shared Room* (Minnesota, 2020), and *Yang Warriors* (Minnesota, 2021).

Kevin Yang is a multimedia storyteller born and raised in the Twin Cities who finds most of his inspiration unraveling his Hmong American experience with others. He creates in the mediums of spoken word poetry and documentary filmmaking. He represented Hamline University at the College Union Poetry Slam invitational and was a New Angle Documentary Fellow at Saint Paul Network.